selected
poems

[TRANSLATIONS]

Philosophy of Surrealism by Ferdinand Alquié. (Ann Arbor: University of Michigan Press, 1965)

Reversal by Claude Royet-Journoud. (Providence, RI: Hellcoal Press, 1973)

The Notion of Obstacle by Claude Royet-Journoud. (Windsor, VT: Awede, 1985)

If There Were Anywhere but Desert: Selected Poems of Edmond Jabès. (Barrytown, NY: Station Hill Press, 1988)

Etat by Anne-Marie Albiach. (Windsor, VT: Awede, 1989)

Ralentir Travaux by André Breton, Paul Eluard, and René Char. (Cambridge, MA: Exact Change, 1990)

Boudica by Paol Keineg. (Providence, RI: Burning Deck, 1994)

Objects Contain the Infinite by Claude Royet-Journoud. (Windsor, VT: Awede, 1995)

Elegies by Jean Grosjean. (Providence: Paradigm Press, 1996)

Click-Rose by Dominique Fourcade. (Los Angeles: Sun and Moon, 1996)

Heart into Soil by Xue Di. Translated with Wang Ping et al.

(Providence: Burning Deck and Lost Roads, 1998)

Prose Poems [1915] by Pierre Reverdy. Center Book in *Untitled*, no. 2 (2001), pp. 55–108

Mental Ground by Esther Tellermann. (Providence, RI: Burning Deck, 2002)

An Ordinary Day by Xue Di. Translated with Wang Ping et al.

(Farmington, ME: Alice James Books, 2002)

Close Quote by Marie Borel. (Providence, RI: Burning Deck, 2003)

Another Kind of Tenderness by Xue Di. Translated with Forrest Gander et al.

(Brooklyn: Litmus Press, 2004)

Theory of Prepositions by Claude Royet-Journoud. (Iowa City, IA: La Presse, 2006)

Zone by Xue Di. Translated with Waverly, Wang Ping et al. (Española, NM: Yefief World Editions, 2006)

An Earth of Time by Jean Grosjean. (Providence, RI, Burning Deck, 2006)

The Form of a City Changes Faster, Alas, than the Human Heart by Jacques Roubaud. Translated with Rosmarie

Waldrop. (Normal, IL: Dalkey Archive Press, 2006)

The Flowers of Evil by Charles Baudelaire. (Middletown, CT: Wesleyan University Press, 2006)

Figured Image by Anne-Marie Albiach. (Sausalito, CA: Post-Apollo Press, 2006)

Paris Spleen: Little Poems in Prose by Charles Baudelaire.

(Middletown, CT: Wesleyan University Press, 2009)

The Whole of Poetry Is Preposition by Claude Royet-Journoud. (Iowa City, IA: La Presse, 2009)

Four Cut-Ups by David Lespiau. (Providence, RI: Burning Deck, 2011)

Four Elemental Bodies by Claude Royet-Journoud (Providence: Burning Deck, 2013)

selected
poems

keith waldrop

OMNIDAWN PUBLISHING
OAKLAND, CALIFORNIA
2016

Original cover collage by Keith Waldrop

Book cover and interior design by Cassandra Smith of Molo Projects
www.moloprojects.org

Offset printed in the United States
by Edwards Brothers Malloy, Ann Arbor, Michigan
On 55# Enviro Natural 100% Recycled 100% PCW
Acid Free Archival Quality FSC Certified Paper

Library of Congress Cataloging-in-Publication Data

Names: Waldrop, Keith, author.
Title: Selected poems / Keith Waldrop.
Description: Oakland, California : Omnidawn Publishing, [2016]
Identifiers: LCCN 2015040781 | ISBN 9781632430205 (softcover : acid-free
  paper)
Classification: LCC PS3573.A423 A6 2016 | DDC 811/.54--dc23
LC record available at http://lccn.loc.gov/2015040781

Published by Omnidawn Publishing, Oakland, California
www.omnidawn.com   (510) 237-5472   (800) 792-4957
10 9 8 7 6 5 4 3 2 1
ISBN: 978-1-63243-020-5

Grateful acknowledgment is made to the editors and publishers of the books in which the poems of this selection first appeared:

A Windmill Near Calvary (University of Michigan Press, 1968); *Songs from the Decline of the West* (Perishable Press, 1970); *Poem from Memory* (Treacle Press, 1975); *Windfall Losses* (Pourboire Press, 1977); *The Ruins of Providence* (Copper Beech, 1983); *A Ceremony Somewhere Else* (Awede, 1984); *Hegel's Family* (Station Hill Press, 1989); *The Locality Principle, The Silhouette of the Bridge*, and *Semiramis If I Remember* (Avec Books, 1995, 1997, 2001); *Haunt* (Instance Press, 2000); *The House Seen from Nowhere* (Litmus Press, 2002); *No: a Journal of the Arts* (2003); *Transcendental Studies* (University of California Press, 2009); *The Antichrist, The Garden of Effort, The Space of Half an Hour*, and *Analogies of Escape* (Burning Deck, 1970, 1975, 1983, 1997).

The following books were originally published by Omnidawn:

The Real Subject: Queries and Conjectures of Jacob Delafon, with Sample Poems End Fragment (2004), and *The Not Forever* (2013).

CONTENTS

FROM A WINDMILL NEAR CALVARY

1968

ANGEL TO LOVE, MAN TO WORLD

I was reared among prophets, who saw
one true Word in a deceiving world and
fixed their gaze on it. I remember (dimly)
stunning silences, and messages — come down
whole from above — and mysteries, in a matrix
like gnashing of teeth.

Now what possesses me? Someone who didn't
know me might take me for a connoisseur —
I stare till I wonder those canvases (for
instance) are not consumed, and expect any day
to see it posted: *défense de manger
les objets d'art.*

It's simple voracity, the garden-of-Eden
chomp. (We see — by and large — what
we want to see. At least that explains
why just looking around us makes us
guilty — by breathing open Adam's eyelid God
damned the mud.)

A shamed child would like, as Erikson
puts it, "to destroy the eyes of the world."
Failing that, he closes his own eyes, tightly.
As for me, I cultivate my field of nothingness
a bit extravagantly. (I know the world exists.
I do not know

how the world exists. I do not know how
I know the world exists. Empty mind
is a greedy darkness. Brightness is
all there is. From a bright point
light pulsates, throb after throb, into the
ravening dark.)

If my retinal sensitivity were increased, I
would perceive, I'm told, not more occult
hills or finer prospects, but irregularities
of the light itself. Strange as it
seems, there's nothing more to see.
(Fabulous world.)

No one thing will do — more and more, nothing
will substitute for anything else. Wrapped
in the accidents of an untasted
apple, even Good and Evil might be appetizing.
And couldn't I regard my death as Eve did hers —
salivating?

I'd like an inclusive mind, where nothing could
possibly be out of the question. Like Saint
Mark's facade where, half way up a
clutter of Christianity and Venetian lace, are
four Roman horses, poised, in place.
Surely it was

thinking like this made Brueghel paint
a windmill near Calvary. When Adam, as it
fell out, got too old to know Eve, he sat
his inspired carcass down by his hoe, watching
his sweaty children screw up generation
after generation.

ANTIQUARY

Some people try, before cashing in, to make
their lives into shrines. Mine seems to be turning out,
as predicted, a small provincial museum, the kind
that might have in some corner or other one work
you could be interested in, if you knew it was there.
Memorials and keepsakes hang around, half catalogued. Some
curiosa, here and there a whopper — who else
could maintain a scarlet nose drinking
Dr. Pepper? I have my precedents. Lots of men
shuffle off, leaving a ball of tinfoil too large to get
out of the attic or half a century of the New York Times
or some other mess. I keep everything. Old
gods and old ads fade together; both
show better on a neutral wall. Philosophies, old hat,
catch dust on a rack. The trouble is
I'm a glutton. The floor is cluttered,
the shelves go across the windows. I trip
sometimes over ancient arguments or
a lid I can't place, or claim two different heads
to be Saint Thomas's. Nothing, nothing will I
surrender. There is little enough as it is.
I may, of course, croak tomorrow, stumbling
from the larder, but I will not set
my house in order.

Conversion

I am already sweeping towards my most
permanent state. Keith means "wind," according
to *What to Name the Baby*. There is
a paradise promised for those who despise
whatever turns — flesh going sour — and I
have despised it.

But I have been converted. Stock dreams can be
flicked on, the assured voice forming first and
then, slowly, its radiant body, but they fulfill
no wish of mine. All my aerier hopes
have dwindled to a momentary point of light,
disappearing.

Reality is what does not change, i.e., reality
is what does not exist, held desperately.
All my past sins I attribute to a
commerce with angels, someone else's. The
earth brings forth of itself and the rest is only
worth a thought.

Now faces crop out of the most random
inorganic patterns, usually nobody's in particular
I take them as a less specific, less
beautiful, Allegory of Spring. Sometimes,
at night, my head swerves in a rising spiral
of labyrinthine

vertigo, descending only in the arc of sleep.
But I have learned to like the dust I am fed by
winds that shift across an actual world.
I am already what I will be later. And the cycles
shorten. I owe letters to so many, I doubt
that I will ever catch up now.

CREDO

It is a great doctrine that says we
believe as much as we deserve. Saint Thomas was worth,
apparently, everything in the *Summa*, though he couldn't stomach
the Immaculate Conception. Mrs. Katache of Arkhangelsk
supposes she's a chamber pot and shrieks to be emptied.
What does one have to do, or be, to accept
streets of gold or the big lift at the Rapture? Perhaps
Gregory, for his compassion, was allowed to imagine sinners
scorching out their stains in Purgatory.
I know a Christian, says she
just has to laugh thinking of all those atheists going to
wake up in hell. There are those for whom God is
dead, but who fear the Devil or my black cat. I think
the time is coming and maybe now is when the tree that
overshadows this house will grow from my forehead, spreading
like veins, ring after ring.

HORROR STORY

I had two
grandfathers. One was a bald gentle postmaster
in Leeton, Missouri; he died and was buried.
The other was some kind of preacher;
I never saw him. The terrible thing about
ghosts is that we know they are not there.
Two grandmothers. One chased me with a
broom because I accused her of riding it.
The other stopped listening and went deaf.
They both survived their husbands, but
now they are both dead. My father is
dead too, but this is no elegy.
I was disappointed early, by lack of precision.
I found it hard to keep a grip
on outlines. They always slip.
The fine delineation swells
around the edges, where it smells.
Woman, be strange, take me with your eyelid.
Nothing in dead landscapes suggests terror.
I have married a wife whose
surface I adore. And other surfaces.
Who knows what may leap out from the shadows?
Loved houses are haunted. And I have
no explanation.

Graven Images

In my neighborhood, even the children
are travelers. The kids I wave to,
because they wait for the school bus
in front of my house, have
some of them lived in three states.
At least one was born in California.

And this is Connecticut, where — I was
warned — a man is a stranger
unless his grandfather is buried here, and
shiftless if his house was not
inherited. Nevertheless, the new over-
hang across the street is posted *For Sale*.

And in graveyards around this Durham,
whose perpetual care lapsed ages ago,
bones borne in wooden boats from Old England
lie packed in plots of rocky dirt,
remembered by slate or granite
slabs that boast a coffin blossoming

or the Archangel with his trumpet or,
oftener, Time snuffing out a candle
or a skeleton or just a simple skull.
Some brat has chalked the word *screw*
at the edge of my drive, and doodled
around it unequivocal hieroglyphics.

From Raymond Queneau

"Je crains pas ça tellment"

That don't scare me so much death of my guts
death of my bones death of my nose
That don't scare me so much me a skeeter sort
baptized Raymond from a line of Queneaus

That don't scare me so much where my books get stacked
in book stalls in johns in dust and doldrums
That don't scare me so much me who scribble a pack
and boil down death into some poems

That don't scare me so much Soft night flows
between ringwormy eyelids over dead eyeballs
Night is soft a redhead's kiss
honey of meridians at north and south poles

I'm not scared of that night not scared of absolute
sleep It must be heavy as lead
dry as lava dark as the sky
deaf as a beggar bellowing on a bridge

I'm scared stiff of unhappiness crying pain
and dread and rotten luck and parting too long
I'm scared of the lardbellied abyss that holds sickness
and time and space and the mind gone wrong

But I'm not so scared of that lugubrious imbecile
Who'll come and spit me on his toothpick point
when I'm down and with eyes vague and placid I'll
have lost my cool to the collecting rats

Someday I'll sing Ulysses or maybe Achilles
Aeneas or maybe Dido Quixote maybe Sancho

Someday I'll sing pleasures the idle know
the fun of fishing or the peace of villas

All fagged out today by the hours as they wind out
trudging like an old nag around the dial
a thousand pardons from this skull — a ball —
for doling out plaintively this song of the void

FROM WINDFALL LOSSES

1977

After Midnight

Sleep lies vaguely in a ring on
the other side of the walls. The furniture
is no defence, dull with stains and
familiar.

If I look very long at the
flame leaping out of that
log, I find it possible to think
that I recognize a world
of things only because all
things exist already in
my mind. External things, that is, may
merely
remind me.

It's possible. I don't usually
think so.

Like a child, I resist
sleeping until
sleep clobbers me unconscious.

I admire a version of the story
of Pygmalion where, the instant Galatea
begins to breathe, she turns out to be
a soprano and she sings, "Where
am I? and
what am I thinking?"

Then there's the tale in
which Adam, just out of the mud, to
prove that he's
alive, sneezes.

But I'd like to think I'm
perfectly articulate in
what I'm suggesting. To any stray
notion one can assign a name or
a number. There's nothing
indistinct about the concept 'vapor.'

Or — start again — what I'm thinking of is
like a house in the
middle of an ill-defined region.

My evidence is a range of curves
strong enough to give an edge
to waves, vibrations, intimations,
influences.

We are all very very
complicated, specialized machines, but we
breathe sleep in
from the common reservoir.

It's very late. The log
has long been ashes. Words, fortunately, can be
jotted, as music is inscribed on rust.

COMMUNICATION

No sooner is the tea into my teacup
and Rosmarie settled comfortably, across
the room, into Proust's world, I
begin this scratching around after some
semblance of elegance.

Does that mean I want
to say something?
I don't think so.

But I confess a hankering after
periodic sentences. Even
while writing some other kind.

As for Earl Grey, whoever
he was, we may assume he preferred
a rough but aromatic brew.

There's an elegant poem by
Swift, on a bride who, unwisely, on her
wedding night has twelve cups of tea.

The kind of tea not specified.

In experiments by Delgado and
others, miniature electrodes
are implanted in the tissues of the living
brain, and precise charges administered
by radio control. Sham-rage, sham-
sex, sham-sleep are all
available by command.

Charlus's love-life with such
a device could have been straightened out.

Maybe also Proust's, and his asthma.
Everyone must have noticed — so
it's nothing much to be saying — how everything
we drink turns to urine. Everything
flows, sooner or later, and the rivers
being, as they are, full of putrid
matter and poison and whatever we've

eliminated, I suggest thinking
twice before stepping in.

Otherwise, for the moment, no
message.

Money

Money
is pure spirit. It's what you convert
things into so as to carry their
value without their weight.

Things, everybody agrees, are
interchangeable. Everything
has its price.

Money is the philosophers'
stone.

In the mind, too, the hard
law holds — everything
must be paid for.

You'd think at some point or
other there'd be an unexpected surplus. One of those
chain letters could
come through with four thousand ninety-six
one dollar bills. You can't deny, some
people do seem to make fortunes from
next to nothing.

I treasure Blake's proverb about
the fountain overflowing and, even more, an old
phrase about "a fountain
of gardens." But I'm
jotting down here, just so
I won't forget, how feelings that
seem timeless pass
quickly out of currency.

Those who think God created heaven
and earth must consider him
Number One Spendthrift. They must
found their hopes on possible
blunders in his accounting.

It's hell to be poor.

Motion Discomfort

El Cheapo in the jaws of Camp
pollutes the pressurized air as we
streak in the general direction
of the Houses of Parliament.

And I am thinking over, in my
vague way, some of the possible relations
between this body, those clouds, that
ocean down there.

I'm a bit uncomfortable, but not
really scared. Nothing, in a realm so
purely conjectural, can actually hurt.

I remember a friend, now, who had always taken
for granted that the toilets on airplanes
were just like train toilets, which open onto
the ties beneath.

I think also how Epicurus taught that
all things, being heavy, fall forever, but
gently, without impact, having no
place to land.

WINDFALL LOSSES

35

My Nodebook for December

for Ihab Hassan

1

Closing the door is supposed to open some
inward source — as with, for example, the prayer-
closet: the text says go in and "shut thy door."
It's a stroke of luck when traditional
wisdom so matches the turning of the season.

2

I've often thought of writing a poem of grotesque
length (an epic, yes) and setting the entire argument
the instant after Gautama's enlightenment, while
it seemed to him he would pass directly
into Nirvana, while the powers of good trembled
thinking man was lost. It was only an
instant, because of course the Buddha
reconsidered.

3

Bulls for the bull-fight must (this is
absolutely essential) be
innocent. The very brightest are certainly,
by human standards, stupid, but
after a few fights the
dullest among them would learn not to
charge an empty cape but turn and
massacre the fancy-pants who dances there
for a bloody crowd. But, as Hemingway

noted, the bull never survives. I can't, myself, get
excited about "life and death, i.e., violent
death," and have never been able to
work up much sympathy for
the brute who runs with his
head down *or* for the show-off, who
has it coming. I'll probably never
develop a taste for battle or
get seven novels written or kill myself.

4

History is hard for me. I've no
sense for it.

5

The world — and if ever there was a self-evident
proposition, here it is — the world
is a big fish. I've caught it in
my net. And now, long into the winter
nights, wearily, I study my net.
The fish stinks.

6

A friend talks passionately in favor of
silence. I listen to him. He says, "Silence
dissolves the categories" and "Silence renews
the potential of consciousness." And it strikes me
that I should say something.
But I've never been able to argue. And whenever there's
been a choice between speaking and keeping still,
I've kept my mouth shut. Well,

usually. And only after
a certain amount of prodding I've
produced the necessary conventional sounds,
feeling the thread of words I spew
inordinately fragile, certainly nothing
to depend on. Whereas the craw of
silence is vast and, anyway,
already has us — it's the scorching sunlight
of a Nilescape or the wind across the Great
Plains, burying us. Friend, waist deep in dust or
sand, maybe we'd contrive a gesture.

7

I passed the peak of my
energy at the age of — it's
hard to believe —
twelve. Since then,
little by little, I've collected
the furniture of my house.
I teach meanwhile, and I
study, but no one knows
my specialty.

8 XMAS [after Pessoa]

A God is born. Some other Gods die. Truth
has neither come nor gone, only the Error has changed.
We have now another Eternity,
and the world is no better off than it was.
Blind Knowing plows a sterile plain
Lunatic Faith lives a dream of worship.
A new God is nothing but a word.
Seek not. Nor believe. All is occult.

9

Time is molecular — so much for
Zeno — and each moment brings everything
out of nothing. In the beginning (each
beginning) the universe is only a
point — no dimension — and then
it's a world, for a moment, and
each moment is apocalypse. *Continuous
creation* it used to be called, and now
we say *expanding* universe because (I
forgot to say) each moment is more. Whatever else it may
be, it's always more. No wonder the poet cries
"Oh, Oh,"
or, on a higher level, lyrical verses. But don't
worry. I'm not violent. We all
live in a residue of
bright pulsations, a gob
of time, an after-image.

10

How naive can you get? — I
was wondering, when the Great
Year comes around to this point again
and the next me sits signing his
poems Keith Waldrop, will he
remember back across the void
of Decembers to where I drift into these
speculations? And a moment's
thought answers my stupid question: I
remember nothing.

11

When I think of the books you could
fill with what I don't know, *oof.* The pressing need's
for a phenomenology of ignorance. Everything has
horizons, and they're not just
out of sight, they loom. Yes, and they beckon.
An open door is plain and simple, like a
wall. A closed door is an invitation. But if
the knob is turning . . . ?
Well, I'm closing in, or opening up. I've been so
bloody finicky the mysteries catch me sometimes
with my lids down. But I'm preparing. I need
many voices for my revenge.

Poem Ending with a Celebration

for Anne-Marie Albiach

I think — well, I
think these real material
machines
are ours. No
progress, I admit, in
supposing that.

It's not a matter of
activity. With practically no
expense of energy, we support
all kinds of signals.

("There are always entities
beyond entities, because nonentity
is no boundary.")

Complicated,
isn't it? But
not tangled.

What I admire most
of all, Anne-Marie (in this 'world' of
letters) is a fine irrational
intelligence.

All connections (all)
connect, not always
as we could want them to.

Therefore: (for you) these
partially organized

bits ("because" is always good
form, as in the construction
"this, well then that").

A celebration along
the lines on which
we're thought.

To Rosmarie in Bad Kissingen

I just squashed a fat
fly who was buzzing me, but he's
more disgusting dead.

If we go by numbers, my old
zoology prof used to say, this
is the age of insects,
more specifically: of beetles.

This is also the age of information.

I hope the churchbells
of Bad Kissingen aren't
keeping you awake — though it's
nice, hearing tones decay. You
won't let the bells chase you to church.

Somebody, just the other day, claimed
that you and I haven't
any roots (he thinks that's bad). It's
true enough that we've fallen between
two generations — one drunk, the other
stoned. The one has
inhibitions to get rid of (you know
what that means: liquor and
analysis); the other, a great
blank space to fill.

The wars of the young I
think will be wars of religion.

But all this letter is really
meant to say is that you should
leave those Kraut Quasimodos at their

glockenspiels and
hurry back here, because whatever we
don't see together has for me always
a dead spot somewhere,

even though I know that one
place is much the same as another,
and all the air we could

breathe anywhere in the world
has already, numberless times, been the
breath of a fern and
a marigold
and an oak.

Two Reports
I (*3 August 1969*)

Nothing is left, Father. Everything
you gave me I've lost or
thrown away. Everything you
tried to teach me I've either
forgotten or never learned.
Only, I still have your watch.

I didn't know you. You were
an old man who appeared at
unexpected moments, day or
night, and went out again
whenever the caller called.
How could I have loved you?

You had hopes for me, and
only didn't live quite long enough
to be disappointed. Well, you spent
half a century before
screwing me up — I must say,
you had no right to expect much.

I rode with you once, on
what you called your waycar and I
still call a caboose. From
Emporia to Newton, or Abilene,
or some other Kansas freightyard.
Now the railroads are dying, Father,

and I'm in Paris, and out my
window there's a half-moon, with
an American flag on it. And
I'm careful not to speak English
in the Vietnamese restaurants. And I hear
your old Hamilton ticking — no, it's mine.

FROM THE GARDEN OF EFFORT

1975

Propositions and Between

PROPOSITION I

Sunlight — yes. I
mean yes it's
there.

*

Things
separate. My
eyes smart.

*

Dark. Indefinite
sounding.

*

Two
knowledges: (1) not to
stumble, (2) not
to move.

*

Look on tip-
toe. Listen
horizontal,
breath held.

*

Under sixty watts. Write:

*

What
can I lure
here

ENTRIES

I was
preceded
by
mine.

*

One interpretation among.

*

Addressed
to a certain
bearing.

*

Following
succeeds.

*

These words on
parole.

The Chapters Together

1

who a high degree

2

who am cry

3

who fruits definitely littlest

4

who head a near the

5

who hidden

6

who himself

7

who interlocking first love false

8

who I say

9

who look

10

who organized a wheel

11

who rainbow receive

12

who rapt a separate oil

13

who spiritual mountain

14

who that is thunder tribulation why

15

who the taken out go child

16

who to harvest

17

who top of

18

who when the is given

19

who who

20

who withstands fullness

The Cake He Typed

1
also in supernatural like

2
close out and dimension

3
cosmic whatever was eaten

4
eagle ultra

5
electricity his bride agrees

6
home in the leave

7
Jezebel systems

8
medical fallen thinking

9
might later before

10
next few exactly predicts

11
psychic tissue allows perfect

12

sickness can miracle

13

someday wilderness ate

14

sooner thinking moon would

15

subtle

16

this is protected for

17

to grow public touch

Muscle Above Mind

engineering mothers
to make of
being born
question to
us all in
the end

*

in the midst
of pioneer
bulk blindness
to now and
again extravagant
strange

*

careful ferocity
priest two nuns
forestalling vulgarity and
heaven simple
Catholic imagery

*

dead at
a funeral great
trouble death
it is
clear now vanity

*

neat narcissism satisfying
lengthier mechanical
parts train naked
eager to impress

*

with exploit
in the full
sense will
but is
not quite

*

comically kicked in
his most
often for fleshly
thinking unlikely

*

great immediate
years short of
suddenly for
the whole room

*

conversations with
men and
women the story
with leaping

*

ascetic in love
with positive
response attachment lived

*

circumambient moment direct
something "and
never really is"

*

dream eyes a
head bound with
real fantastic

*

looking obsessed to
forget and
neglect could concern

*

here seated
by body mad
in my

*

house cannot
move the this
bit housing

*

nicely claustrophobic
man shedding
England soon elbow

*

changing qualifications
seated the
animal images

*

reshuffled to
recover all the
· forms
                *

stiff stuff an
occasionally sleeps

*

mistake about
the stone

*

pity coming the
finished

*

quiet extensive
stretch of

PROPOSITION II

Each grain of sand has its architecture, but
a desert displays the structure of the wind.

A Hatful of Flood

1

Outside the calendar,
werewolves and other
danger spots.

*

Almost everybody, you
know, is dead.

*

Teeth, nails and
hair — what a moving
landscape.

*

Two segments of
horizon, haggling
over a birthday.

2

Am I a prisoner?

*

Pumpkins, by
gouging, given
eyes, nose, grin.

*

Remember me only
by what I've
said in my sleep.

*

Corridors and boxes, swell
of little cells.

*

Empty? Filled?

*

Time. The fatness
of time.

3

A face at the
window and I forget
I'm indoors.

*

Their language, in
so many senses.

*

I, a region
of you, a
region of me.

*

Our system un-
stable — evidence
in time.

*

Enormous eyes of
Christians or
decadent pagans.

*

Some things I've
seen through and
vice versa.

*

Worth everything
but not necessarily
worth while.

*

In different
groupings, an
instant, as if it
were an instant.

*

Not bodies, but
"entities
carefully abstracted."

*

The unlived life is
not worth examining.

4

What happens
at the exact
center?

*

Consciousness
merely the
environment.

*

Pianos, complex
as they are, not
to be considered
our rivals.

*

I remember
everything and it's
all wrong.

*

Jump ahead and
no one is alive.

*

Convergence
to a web:
nearer, farther.

*

Nearer.

5

Bonelike light, straining
in patterns
of a dozen arbitrary
figures.

*

Half expected.

*

Fading — I'm
dredging, between
dreams.

*

The obscurer
euphemisms. Gossip
of kindergartens.

*

My proper
doorstep, and a
shadow, face down.

6

Absence as
object of fetish.

*

History recuperating.

*

Sick with
reminiscence, unless
I remember.

*

Discovering a
dead end. Go on
and conjecture.

*

The vague
concept of
arrival.

*

In broad
daylight, there were
no more symptoms.

7

Joy and pain
rejoice the
soul, being
physical.

*

The better games the
hard ones.

*

A sense of
tricycling
through the void.

*

Or, at least, a
chance of losing.

*

And, well yes, even
if broken,
rules.

8

What carol, what margin
of error can compare
with the history of France?

*

From one corner of
the hall even
to the other.

*

The earth — such
suspense.

*

Various more or less
recondite linguistic
problems or tea.

9

Your body poses
no problem.

*

Still on the surface.

*

This an
occasion of lucidity.

*

You reflect. You
scatter.

*

Flowing
light, your outline.

*

It takes a
moment to
see you.

*

The sunniest embrace
radiates vagueness.

    *

Elementary spectre.

    *

Play, our
symmetries.

    *

Otherwise
clear, dark.

10

Starting
from 'here.'

*

A look in all
directions, not — to be
sure — at once.

*

The garden of effort.

*

The damned
cannot say
'now.'

1970

The Antichrist

This tube is blind in front
and behind. On the mountain above it
are fine remains, an
unworked concession
of copper, silver and lead. The two,
indeed, react on one another.

Then, on that
night, the
enumerator
revisits his beat. (See LADYSMITH.)

Here the inconsistency becomes
manifest. He had almost daily
intercourse with
Mirabeau. He
studied for the church, but
declined to sign a religious formula. He was
an enthusiastic admirer of J. S. Bach.
What has become
of the herds of wild oxen? A wild, fierce
people paint their
bodies and go naked.
Coleridge recommended some such method of criticism.
One dies on the average each
year, till all are gone

Introducing a Madman

He finished his speech in a
gruesome way. Ha! Ha!

I can feel it wet round
her neck, for now
both mother and daughter lay in it, more
radiantly beautiful than ever.

Introducing a madman: My God!
what has happened to him?

Crush me with fear and
horror, you so
clever lady (with a
strength which seemed incredible).

FROM THE SPACE OF HALF AN HOUR

1983

Poem from Memory

for Jaimy Gordon

"A lost notion, then, which we have entirely
forgotten, we cannot even search for."

Saint Augustine

If one
smokes, there
is the burnt
match, the
butt,
the ashes. There are
crusts, crumbs, spit
out pits. There
is body.
I recall my
body, because it is
present.
And because I
reach out, sifting
ruins for
old manuscripts.
The sense of
the past
springs from
familiarity with
already things. Faces
with nothing new,
stale
objects, received
communications. The
sense of the
present also.
Presentiments appear out of
a dark ground, a

nudge of
sexual fluids. I've
been looking for
you. Everywhere. In
all the obvious
moments, but also
along odd
interfaces.
My father used to
go into
a rage, if anything
was misplaced. Anger
was his order.
It seems fitting we
leave his grave
unmarked, who
always said, when he
could think of
nothing else to say,
"Well, it's
this
world, and
then the fireworks."
Where
are you?
Associations
are not free.
Geographical, we
extend into the
cosmic. But in stepping a few
steps backwards, I'm
in a different
space, precarious.
As when the statue
descends a fourth.
As you
haunt me with

melodies, un-
placeable because somewhat
mis-sung. The year I
was born gave
birth to monsters.
And every year.
It is possible,
even likely, that
there is no center.
Eternity is
simply time
without us. Before
or after. One has
only the choice to
pick
or to dance.
We dream
before birth.
Perhaps you
inhabit
the desire-body. And
while my
grosser faculties
sleep, you
hover above
the sleeper, sleepless.
And
unrepressed. Show
me, in dreams I
won't remember,
the hell prepared for
sins I've forgotten.
This model has
something
to be said for it.
Every
where is ribbed

with feeling, mixed
emotions.
Childhood, when
the teeth are planted,
overgrown with luxuriant
imagery. My
senses remain
local, but reply with
the universal slang.
At the end of
the world, can
I still stretch out my
hand? I
take one skip at a
time, learning
by terror, always
elsewhere. Between thumb and
index finger, primordial
void. Nothing
remains. Why
should you?
Unthinkable
spaces propel us
into time. And always
the doorbell. My
latest recollection
interests
me least of all.
Nothing helps unless
I can deal
it out of order.
My reminiscences
alter, as the
débris of fall
differs from
spring's débris.
Impulses

pass, strewing
dead pathways.
"Oh I just
wonder," says my
mother, "will
the circle be un-
broken." As
if the statement
were its whole
development, you
hide your energy.
A storehouse
could not
contain such over-
lapping. It is
arguable that I
merely reason
from the present back to
some representation,
just as certain
possibles
present themselves
now.
Then the code tells
all, and
is altogether secret.

                    *

Meaning should be
understood, like a
missing Buddha
surrounded by appearances.
I think I
hear distant
waves, though not
sure just

what waves at this
distance would sound like.
Continuity
insists I
fail to move. Rhythm is
stifled by time. My dreams
are experimental.
I need disguises.
Cell-destroying thoughts.
Fossil waters.
"Bell turds." A long
enchantment, like offering
tobacco to the sun.
My relation to
the glass of
water on the
table in
this house at such
and such co-ordinates is
one of thirst and
possibility. I live
in ghost states, caressing
imaginary substances. Moments
smear. You
compare with
clouds, tidal
disturbances, rising and
dissolving across
a field. But
not entirely
favorably. To
live longer in
each instant, as certain
birds are
said to do, would
change a constant
pitch

to pulses. The slightest
backward
glance and things
cave in. What
hope for whispers, when
evening is broadcast?
Everyone
on the warpath. Me
too. Killed, and it was as
if I had
merely stumbled.
My wife, my
wife would not
look at me.
It occurred to
me that I was
dead, and sure
enough, I
spotted my body.
You cannot imagine how
hungry birds are,
always. *My*
friend, we
have been killed.
For lack of
everything, I
image anything. In the
shadow of
old analogies. Tunnels
nowhere. All notes struck
from a single string
stretched infinitely.
I waver between
map and
territory, time
and eternity. I
count on a

steep forgetting curve,
unlearning by
interference,
by decay. Tracks
fade. Betweens
come clear. It's
cheaper to let
old rails remain,
a network under
later asphalt.
The layers
communicate. Not a
day goes by, but it
insists on being recorded.
Uncalled for, un-
noticed, there
you are still, with
Jericho's leveled
defences, buried
motives, types of arche-
ology. Lacking in
measure, poor
in grace. It isn't
that I know
anything worth
comment. My only
hope is that I'll
know it when
I see it. What could
reduce a man
to traces?

*

I only know where it
is I'm looking
from what I'm

looking at. Objects
thin into
etymologies. I see
by getting about. I
remember by wanting, eyes
in perpetual
movement.
the future is a
long retrospective, watching
a whole
life pass. The law of
accident assumes the
certainty of error.
Current models
stand in a series of
static displays. Someday
I will forget even
my obsessions. All
souvenirs are phony.
In my train of
thought, the scenery
extends for miles,
stripped of breath.
Augustine had a friend who
could recite the *Aeneid*
backwards. Perfection
demands images at
strategic intervals, something
steady on which to
map at random. My world
is in disorder. Like-
wise my schedule. I
live within
acceptable
tolerances. At the
intersection of innumerable
fantasies. Irreconcilables

point me to
my orient. Ambiguous
suns. A shower of
elementaries. Venus rising
from the nutrient broth.
Accidents of sensual
logic. Fringes of
interference. That
doorbell. My path
is undeterminable, through
areas that
fail. Vague
reliefs. Fog at the borders. The frontier
viscous. In a rage at
being named,
the animals tear them-
selves in two. I reconnoiter
the universal momentary,
a spirit traveling for
self-improvement.
Free or directed,
I step from one
messge to another, at
the boundary between
masks. Death
distracts from various sensible
speculations
on the cocktail
party problem. I think I'm
done with, well for
example, trains and
in an unguarded
moment the
tracks cross my mind.

*

Something is always
pulling, little
balloons full of
sentences. By spurning the
world, my
eyes created me. And each
new sight argues
outward, dead against
circumference. Already
keyed for my
coming, a complex
hierarchy cannot
not communicate. My knowing with-
draws, unknowable, amid
widening rings of
devastation. A sphere
of torment. Pain
expanding. My
face, partially
controlled, contains in
its sounds and silences the
real substance.
Long ranges
curve into bodily
changes. Strains
develop I've never heard
of. Buddha may
indulge in a trace of
smile, but
not laugh. Jesus
blubbers. Individual
things are
real enough. It's only
the sum of things
that's false. Balsa
sawdust on a
vibrating membrane shows

where the force
hinges. Any dream at
all produces an
erection. Explanations
beg for questions,
authorize
versions. I
swallow, but it's
more than enough.
There's some priceless
thingamajig
lost, maybe, because I
keep guard, dragoning
ancient treasure, heaping
around me the
symbols of experience. Green
mist. The cold
gray dawn. Fireflies
among city dwellings. Through
the seasons there are
feasts, festivals. At
night, secretions. I carry
always my blest
cloth. One never
knows when. Units of
account cancel stores
of value. Fear of
infancy is a
donation to the adults.
To take by
lips what survives
in kissing. We
deal with extreme, even
violent hunger. The
tendency to re-
turn, a foreign
body, in

the form of
disgust, close
accord, a well-
defined impasse. The stomach
responds continuously.
Every few years somebody
comes up with Noah's ark, on
one or another
god-forsaken mountain, not
always Ararat. Whatever is
moving is
obviously in the now.
How can I be certain these
are only
machines? The more I
reject, the bigger
my alternative becomes. Furniture
in profusion. Baroque
gaze into exploding
crystal.
The dream is
asleep. There are
other layers. I
am playing with
a woman's breasts.
Partial
awakening. Sucking
order, but
too dark to
concentrate.
Magic, it
turns out, is
only a mnemonic.
The standing
sleeper, there's a
clear-cut
position. Sensations of

tone require a world-
view to sustain. Memory
breaks down to
memories. Local
divergencies. I'm looking for
the last number. The
devil's there
somewhere, back of
temporary surfaces. If I
scratch far enough, I'm bound to come
down with something. The
doorbell. The doorbell. And also
the phone rings constantly.
Sexual imagination, derived
from the closed eyes.
Where are you? Where
on earth. I see
everything mine
distance, become
environment. My house, my
room, my body, mind,
my inmost self. A universe
in whoosh. "Postponement
of understanding." Farther and
farther the finer
the analysis. But no
center. Only vectors of
rejection, lines
of force. Thus
reach.
Open.
Secret.

ELEGY

"He comes to himself, like a gift."
Karl Jaspers

i

This body, mine, is only
an image of my brain, which
spreads fan-like its systems of

control. Thirty-six feet
under the terrace
of the Thames, three

fossil bones have been unburied:
an occipital and two
parietals, which articulate perfectly

together — a woman, in
her twenties probably,
from the space between

two ice ages. It's
possible to think of an infinity
limited to one

dimension. Her face, of
course, is lost, though certainly she
carried her head erect. These

fragments of a skull
are dressed out scrupulously now, for
purposes of study. Like a

vanity. Around her, we may suppose
animals — some long since
extinct — and a whole
range of expression: gestures,

sounds, some of which
still echo, perhaps, in our

emotions. Meanwhile, all
legends about roses
bleed them from white to red.

ii

Saint Michael, as he flashes his
sword, should sweat. That he doesn't
is a sure sign that the great
Enemy, no longer a menace, has
nothing to fear. It's against
us — to win us over — that Michael turns the
blade just so. We so often make

the old mistake: supposing the body
'inhabited'
by soul, self, what you will. Whereas, in fact, the
cinnamon bird brings us cinnamon
and we haven't any idea where
the cinnamon grows. This account is
etched on my sleep, no amount of

wishpower will unprint it. You,
if you were young, might
glisten like olive oil. But rough
to the eye and to touch, wrinkled and
skilled, we stride the length and
breadth of the garden. There is a message
which holds the flesh to the bones — and

another one: *splash blood*
on the lintel and on
the posts of the door and stay
inside. Because once the Destroyer has
permission to destroy, he
does not distinguish between
the righteous and the unrighteous. Any evening,

with the falling temperature, dust
descends, altering every surface on

earth: hair falls, and silk,
and the silk also of spider webs. Organisms
complex and tiny beyond imagining
float invisible in the invisible air where knife-
shaped particles redden the sky with

a red they themselves do not
possess. The soul keeps
its distance. I will not discuss
the angel Murmur, who
teaches philosophy, or the likelihood
of a new ice age, or that pair of
slippers worn by Enoch before the flood.

iii

Put into perspective, the dome
of the State House sinks,
draws together on itself, and becomes
obscure. It narrows, progressively, as I
move away from it, up the hill or

through the years. A glacier moves
with the same motion as a river, only
more slowly, sides dragging
against the boulders and débris of its
banks. We are all held in the

coffin of space. If I carry a stone
from Michigan to Rhode Island, is that
less 'natural' than transport by
glacier? — though ice would hardly
have pushed it this direction. Clear

crystals, some have claimed, redden and glow
into rubies, perfection at no
price, in an eternity of un-
timed processes. All day, today,
the thought of blood has

bothered me, appearing in the periphery
of my mind's eye. It surges into
the field. There is no
help for it — attention will
center on that fluent

red, as it will on any
alien substance. Imperfect fluids, viscous
bodies, are urged down certain in-
clinations by the natural
pressure of their parts. Here comes

glory: sludge within
sludge, strain-centers
in a medium with
all the properties of unannealed
glass. Thinking, like

wind that builds and then
dies down, takes
time. Do you believe
in change? This is a place
almost impossible

to leave. Three men, poured by an
avalanche into a crevasse
at the foot of Mont Blanc,
were found, forty years later, miles
downstream, still in solid

ice, coming closer and closer to the
surface. On my one hand,
stasis — on the
other, striving for effect. Break a
twig from a long dead elm, blood

branches from the act. No
image escapes, forked lightning or
lake. At times, I must admit, I
take the nearest objects — anything at
all — for comfort, for defence

against an empty field, the vacant
air. But other times, the spaces between things
all but make up for the intervening
entities. Point-instants, I
remind myself, are nothing, from

nothing. There is not much
time for me to
take. If everything behaved
exactly as I want it to, it
might as well be

all in my head. In my
brain is a constant
gray, cancelling silence. I only
glimpse, where they run at un-
certain depths, blue veins. Skim through

the alphabet. You'll see
how the letters follow their set
order, like the formula for some
catastrophe, called forth by
accident, irreversible.

iv

Sorrow and love, in the old hymn, flow
mingled down. There are times when you
realize you're lost by seeing something
you recognize, some known configuration that couldn't be
where you thought you were. I notice
now and again, how messianic themes
darken the clearest thought, spilling
blood and water across simple
vistas. The Creation is definitely

unfinished. The largest motion — to, fro,
up, down — collapses to a steady but
painful vibration, symmetrical like a
web around the fabulous notion
of 'center.' What I describe
is the region inside these lines which, being drawn,
pattern the interplay of nerve
and muscle. Each effort
surpasses and inscribes its

aim. To reach past the table is to
try for totality, the whole
terrestrial plane. If I forget
you, my memory has not
failed me — it has provided knowledge of
endless loss. Crystals driven downward
drift into impassable peaks. There is a second
air, finer than air, all-pervasive, riddling
the world and supporting the subtle

orders. The righteous are unredeemable, possessed
as they are by their own good angels. Under the
mask the image develops and
through the image, as a goal,

all the colors of the natural world, mixed
and not altogether comprehensible. Everything grows
heavier, at least I do, and — not to surrender
the high tone of gravity — the universe
displays a degrading shift towards red.

V

Lips meet: spirit
breathes into
spirit, or a vague mist
forms. Hardly anything matters to me now
but work, which will be accomplished — if
accomplished — neither by hand nor by
fire, but through its own heat, other
heat serving only to ward off

the cold. Red sandstone near
Shrewsbury bears impressions of raindrops — the rain
of an age inconceivably remote. One can even
tell from what direction the shower
fell, which impressed the sandy surface. I
will sleep soon, not in order to rid myself of
consciousness, but to rejoin partial and
impossible objects outlawed by the will to go

on. The creature left dry on the sleeve of a
drying ocean, who developed
breath in defence against a world of air,
although that creature has grown to think
my thoughts, circulate my
blood — still,
I live on the surface, in
a world not yet

evolved. I am not trying to express
anything, only to
sound my way from tones
to other tones. A gesture
may also be a signature. When I last
thought about it, I thought
that perhaps too much emphasis has been put
on both pity and terror.

vi

While she was holding forth (Madame
Blavatsky) a shower of
roses fell from the empty air. Or so it's
recorded. Recorded

likewise: that Madame was as
startled as everyone else. Sometimes I
wish my sense of theater were
less extended. Memories of

mere tone form a dark but active
screen in front of what must have been
real events, things that
happened, in the same

way that the Garden of Eden
flourishes over failures
of recall. In the same way,
we take the world apart for

lumber, only to find
not enough boards for a bookcase,
or else no nails. To take on the power
of an animal — for

instance, a bird's faculty
of flight — one must first
develop that particular animal's
appetite. The perspective here

is askew, without guarantee of
communication with any out-
side, where we might stand or maybe
walk. The strength of the state

gleams in the evening like a
tall empty helmet. If I needed
help, what hill would I climb or
lift my eyes toward?

vii

I would not want to waste what
little I know of
whatever, but it continually
escapes me, driving home like
rain. Mystics know many
ways to sit, masters of still

gymnastics. Then too, my days
scatter off into conversations, classes,
idle chatter and other facets
of hunger. I must learn to consider the
areas I walk through as
unpeopled — dense growth

has got to become a medium
for reflections. How else remember
what otherwise is only
memorable? Like the dead in *All
Hallows Eve* who haunt the places they
always haunted, but now

as if alone. There are three
evil destinies: to be
an animal, a demon, a hungry
ghost — evil because all these are
hungry, and remain so. A candle in a
pumpkin skull brings to the door

polite East Side children dressed
as ghosts, demons, beasts of
prey. On the other hand, one
is made up as a butterfly, monstrous,
like a blaze, among dead
leaves and the wooden

houses. It's hard to imagine these
bodies made of mind — but requiring, just to
function, a world of
resistances. By an advanced technique, one
can contemplate a duplicate
of oneself, within one's own body, and

draw it forth. The hermit Rolle
felt such fire in his breast he put his
hand there to check. Whom do I know
scorched by the spirit? Many years ago,
I wanted to write about
prayer, but was hindered by centuries of

practice — also my religion
got in the way. Am I finally ready? More
likely, such impulses, fading like printed
pages left in sunshine, will have to
be satisfied by abstract surfaces, which
spread as we pull away from them.

viii

Some gods are too high to be
petitioned — either altogether sublime or just

too *good*. Replaced, particle by
particle, bone, under favorable

conditions, retains its original
minute structures, as in life, though

not alive. For flesh to be
preserved is rarer, though

mammoths, found frozen in Siberia, have
still both hide and hair. There are two

times, the prospect of which provides
no posssibility of hope: before

and after. The most common form
of fossil is simply a space where

some creature was. If I had my
prayer, I'd be replaced, moment

by moment, by some harder
activity, something formal enough

that one wouldn't feel one had to
look for meaning. You, if from a distance you

recognized, for instance, my way of
walking, could run to meet me.

Around the Block

I will go for a walk before
bed, a little stroll to settle
the day's upsets. One thing always
follows another, but
discretely — tree after
telephone pole, for instance, or
this series of unlit houses. One moment follows
another,
helplessly, losing its
place instantly to the next. Each frame
fails, leaving behind
an impression of motion.

As for death, at the moment I
think it strangely overrated.

Who now could build
houses like these? who
could afford to? They loom
in the evening of the
East Side, memory-traces
of sometime wealth. Dust
seems forever settling, but
must somehow recirculate.

Once around the block
will do. Porch after porch projects
its columns, seeming one dark and
continuous dwelling. And fear continues,
eternal night shuttering each
source of light. How
remarkable, how remarkably
pleasant, not to be
asleep, still discriminating
dips in the sidewalk, reading
the differences between shadows.

INTERVALS

1

Gradually to compose
you, I think against my
thought, freezing in its

flight an
idea of praise. it will

bear you out, I
hope. Also, I would like
to imitate, but

perfectly, the pitch
of quiet nights.

2

Silence in heaven strikes
common tones. Between
you and me,

one pinpoint of light is
much like another, never

mind the years that
divide them. They do
nothing to establish

the coordinates of
our walk.

3
When once the earth is
gone, God will separate
light from heat,

reserving
the heat for those in hell

and for his saints the
cold light of
love eternal. Within otherwise

"normal" scales, we
are allowed shades.

4
I disorganize my
lines to realize
your tempo. Trapped

in survival mechanisms, I
shift continually the order

of what might happen — events
change character with
each pull towards

unison. Where nothing is
noted, we rest.

5

What is your relation to
my fault? I see your
left on my right, although

we move in concert. Below the surface
great cypresses are submerged, until

one may canoe among
the branches — new lakes, waterfalls
on the level, crevices of unmeasured

depth. Are we anchored in
ordinary questions and answers?

6

It is not as if
we ever chose this
tune. Disease

runs within the
wood, damaging

perfect outlines. To
exalt a valley, some
mountain will be debased. I

step unevenly,
between terminals.

7
Our shadow
strains, as if to be
off on its own — grasps, an instant,

each tree we pass. How
much of

us is in-
volved in its
tumbling

shape? There are leaps,
unpredicted intervals.

8
Pauses consolidate a
rhythm one
might, rushing, mis-

place. "Sureness"
is not the same as

"knowing." I appreciate a tissue
like *to be,* a
certainty like

the wave against Lapland,
a cadenza like ruins.

9

Before I go, let us
put our horseplay in order. This
trope (or

conversion) will
serve its turns. Tonic to

tonic, but what
possibilities of divergence
between

here
and there.

10

A map of expected intensities will
disregard fallen and
splintered

trunks. We follow
the grain, not seeking

to make statues laugh or
dogs sing. We do not
avert our eyes or fear

a second, more hazardous,
glance. Are we near the focus?

11
Every spirit is
winged, angel and
demon alike, and may be

transfigured merely, never made
happy. I muddy

clear ideas, hurrying
to the surface. Physical
harmonies are

at our disposal, simultaneously
theater and thought.

12
Days lose their full
emptiness if we
forget to

measure them. Above profound
features, lines on water connect

continents. Voices
unite
in the silence after

the score. It happens
and it is over.

Range

> ...the endless street, the street that stretches
> beyond the range of the eye...
> — Giedion, *Space Time and Architecture*

Elmgrove Avenue disappears, not
in darkness or
mist — which, Lord knows, there's
plenty of in Providence — but simply
because in eight or ten blocks it
curves. Of course, if I
turn around, this end (my
end) of the street is
clear. On that corner over there,
Lovecraft was born in his
grandparents' house, long
gone, facing Angell.

Elmgrove's
no Bismarckstrasse, nothing
to compare with Broad-
way or State Street, let alone a
thirty-mile stretch in Los
Angeles. The boulevards of
Baron Haussmann are some of them
longer — all wider, more haunted.

But I cannot see to the other end
of Elmgrove, to Swan Point
Cemetery with its late
Victorian angels (you see, I
know they're there) and Lovecraft's
grave and many more elaborate
markers, bearing their inscriptions Lord
knows where, beyond all memory.

The Ruins of Providence

Two oaks — in the afternoon, if
the sun is shining — cast their
shadows across Elmgrove
Avenue. Whether or not there was ever

a grove, the elms are gone.
Gone, too, in Kansas, though I
remember them luxuriant. The electric
company has hacked away

at the maple in front of my
house — chopping an airway
for their power — and it will
blaze yellow and red again this fall, but

I think it is dying. The sycamore in
back, still, sheds its bark
and shines. At least I will not
die in Kansas. Around the corner,

there are two gingko trees, fifteen
feet or so from each other — of different
sex, I suppose. It's hard to know
what to predict or even to prefer

for this terrain: oak forest like
primeval Europe, or endless gingko
grove. I love these wooden houses that
the rich built, and we live in.

71 ELMGROVE AVENUE

Here, and in St. Petersburg, one
dreams of being run over by
horses in the street. St.
Petersburg, Russia, that is, at the
turn of the century. Since the Revolution,
they are more and more (horses, I
mean) a thing of the past — or of
westerns. Which brings me
to Italy, where a torrent of traffic
rushes, honking, over
the Roman Empire. But here,
and through a desert, anytime, the Nile
flows like a dream.

FROM A CEREMONY SOMEWHERE ELSE

1984

An Excellent Guide

1

Body movement will
be scattered pieces
which all
follow. Children learn
relevant motions. (These
efforts worked,
but this
conception is desirable.)

2

Unsure health without
dire consequences
is, to
be sure, nothing.
(The last statement
was necessary.) So
much energy
to deliver.

3

Many in one,
a number, two,
almost a third.

4

(Somewhat obscure.) Ten
years of vital
necessity will be
enough toilet
training. A child's

mastery has a
gift for strength.

5
Quite a tale ebbed and
flowed, "villages of
the simple" undergoing
a "softer' orientation.
A rehash is
their challenge.

6
An important, a
very important, a
frightening, a cataclysmic,
a frantic, a
good and evil
number. A
unique, a single
knowledge is already
possible. The
upsurge is desire.

7
(Enough to turn,
left sleeping on
the hot
grave. Almost everything
has a
rare gift.
Not
water down smoothly,
not empty green.
A new thesis.)

FALLING IN LOVE WHILE ASLEEP

At the ridge, a change
of reflection. The clear
line of coast does not
know its own boundary,
facing, as it
does, wave after wave of
wash. This is
a world already
discovered, a presupposed
world. It's not easy to know
whom not to trust. I
am divided,
shaped,
moved. I
have been decided
in advance. Seeing one, two,
three, past six imagination
gives up, invents
a word for
whatever it intends. I
put my line
down where it's funny, around
discrepancies of one,
two, three. You
are the expression for my
bare statement, establishing and
destroying the
distance
between us. Here,
alongside everything
and nothing. Past
this moment that
turns a weird
angle, the most subtle

corner, something must
crouch. Its absence
quickens the background.
It will appear, if
at all, in a moving
figure, out of a
desolation, a fog of
waste. Dignity
circumscribes our
area. We're on
debatable ground. Existence
becomes terrible when there are
no discoveries, only
revelations.
Defend me.
Rows of digits
draw their
conclusions until not a
lineament remains. I
know you by your
shadow. You approach in
indirections. Worlds near
the center refuse
my grasp, though I
remain apprehensive. A
hair-line crosses
one after another the
objects
once my concern. It
hardly matters what last
word I
manage, since probably I'll
be remembered and
certainly be
forgotten. The fovea
clears trivia. The pictures I
wait towards

form on the mist, projections of
wreckage, sunken junk. We're
coming together from
adjacent
points, along
conjectural lines on supposed
planes. How can I
take my eyes off? We
undergo, each, the
fear of loss and fear of
collision, of being thrown,
ultimately,
away. The onion-layer lens
produces a sharp
image, but around the image
fuzz. What direction can I
threaten? An endless unlistened-to
white sound stretches
along the shore. What was
thought to be Truth helping
Time to lift the Veil
seems now more likely
Night
obstructing the process. I
waive certain
possibilities of being. Who's
behind me, keeping
tabs? Is he
checking for the public records, or
for the tables of some
company? Noise
is always present, even in
the eyes. I
am taken by the edge
that, however
blunt or keen, defines
to that degree a

surface and
raises suspicions of
some depth. A complete
worldliness is
available on the level
of microcosm. I
love songs that
outrun their text and fill
in with fa-la-la or
all the names of the
seasons and
the stars.
A precise law moves
the tides
approximately. To see one's
own death, where
streams flow upstream and mirrors
mirror the opposite
of image, would
require an eye
at our rear end. I
count my words, those
wounds always
closing, always raw. My
waking memory is
not remarkable. This
is a world as
given. I
have refused
all remedies but
you. At the
ridge, sharp, the light
insists on
rapid movements, one-
two-three, the only
answer to
endless curves.

In ridiculous services I
have uncovered my
defences. My laugh-lines
are not explained. I am
not yet figured
out.

How to Tell Distances

Proclus rises from the
surface of the moon, between
fecund and serene
seas, both dry. Long
corridors and unexpected
rooms. One hears
the voice of the page,

aware of bosom. Emphasis
on the simple solids. All our
decorations temporary, dry
panels, friezes.
A side gate promises
unconsidered scenery. We spread
into definitions.

*

You are welcome to this
map, though it does not
begin to chart the necessary
roads to any real event.
What is a cause in
general? All the elements of the
universe, with the single exception
of yourself. Most poems, later
or sooner, go unread. I measure
things by my own
change of place. Intense original
heat gradually
radiating into empty
space. Note Leibniz Mountains.

*

Ghosts of authorities. All
one and all not-one. Mermaids and
dragons, goat-footed Pans, statues
that move without contact. The structure
of the cosmos and the
structure of Greek
logic both distant as

the moon. Some symbols intelligible
only to the gods. A last
something. Let me put this finally
in your hands. Disintegration, if
on all levels at once, is
positive. it's touch and go.
Gifts are brief, unaccountable.

THE UNTOLD WITCH

1
She would
sigh, if she
could think of
anything intolerable.
Her numbers
fold, in
planes she can
not describe.
Does she
close her eyes for
that faint
red of processes?
Come to me,
by instinct or
for mathematics'
sake.

2
She
moves
in a metaphor of
action.
Heaven, she
says, is
hell
remembered.
Outside her
gaze, I'm
stranded
on fraudulent heights.
No
tune I
know is far
enough out.

3
Man is a matter of
walking
upright, but she
suggests happiness.
Her whole
power
is on the side
of vagueness.
Everything I
need to
know about her is
just before me.
What
can I learn
that is not already
gone?

4
Mountains rule
the world because
she's
from the hills.
When she stands
perpendicular to the
sun's rays, her
light is confined.
If she
turns,
the objective
weakens.
We shall not all
rise, but
all
be modified.

5
I see her
long after
she has
gone away.
There are whole
systems
she
doesn't respond to.
If you
look long enough
everything
is hydraulics.
Out of a
series of partial
images, she is the
one that detaches.

6
If I could
remember
her, we
might build.
Will my
words be fan-
tastic enough to
count?
Whatever
happens now, we
have been
opposite.
Please believe me,
I would
seek you if I
had the distance.

7
Given
time and
invention, she
will surface.
She will
scratch,
meditate, and some
story will suffer.
I refuse to
believe
things unsupported *necessarily*
fall.
She deprives my
dreams
of un-
reality.

8
The hardest
step to take is
always the
next.
She is written
across
her
face.
We are
what we
are, momentary
coincidence.
She is
body,
speaking
through body.

9
She will claim, for
instance, King
Solomon planted
baobabs in India.
And it
may
be
true.
A fine long
rain
penetrates farther
than storms.
Food is
necessary
and
 also logic.

10
Sometimes I'm
angry, and
not at
anything in particular.
She has
seven
divisions, but
no borders.
I could
change your name, since
you always
wanted to be fictional.
Another
unsolved
dream, under
the bridge

11
She has, it would
seem, no
natural
inclination to rise.
She is
whatever I
cannot get
rid of.
She's whatever
refuses
to be
information.
She is my
absence,
my only secure
reference.

12
Just when I'm
ready to let
go, satisfaction
is satisfaction.
Curious text, where
we're
commanded to *acquire*
Nirvana.
Nothing but
impatience
could prompt our
abrupt recognition.
She says virginity
of the mind
can be
restored.

13
Let me
not praise
her past her
due.
She is
a heap of
pebbles
in exquisite random.
Her laughter
rings
empty, where there
were crowds.
My arms
around
you, my
love, are phantoms.

14
She appears sometimes
to be talking
about
other data.
It is as
if she
knew a separate
category.
I tell
her, weeping's
no proof
of the resurrection.
All
of her is
curved
and alters.

15
She can
only
be pictured
as catastrophe.
She con-
fuses
concepts with
irony.
Her thought spreads,
like
children
running home.
She
finds comfort in
the most outrageous
limbs.

16
The moon, according
to her, is
a symbol
for shine.
Residues
provide the
passion
of thought.
Her reflexes
condition
my
mythology.
She is the
energy
of my
indexes.

17
When she
snarls at
me, my
senses sharpen.
Who could expect
her,
without
lying?
She is a
color
outside
the octave.
Her rituals
divide my
life
from its labors.

18
She makes
the right
answer
sound foolish.
The righteous
glory
in their un-
certainty.
Two
nuts represent
us in
divination.
The only
thing she
comes home in
is twilight.

19
She sits
in the
street, making
detours.
Her history is
rich
in in-
decisions.
She is
present,
inclusive,
untransformed.
I do not
pretend
to know
how the flood came.

20
A hymn
describes the
monotony
of her expectations.
She was
created
from the sweat
of peacocks.
Children
defend themselves
with shame
and experience.
All her
objects
answer to the
same name.

21
Better a blank
wall than
simple
dark.
The play in
her muscle de-
termines
where my eyes focus.
She
sleeps at   .
the curve
of my spine.
She wouldn't
believe
me, if I
were to tell her.

FROM HEGEL'S FAMILY

1989

Six Further Studies

I

In heaven there is no more sea, and houses no longer need a widow's walk. And no more widows, there being neither marriage nor giving in marriage. How the air hangs lower and lower on this — I hope — hottest day of summer. A faintly rotten scent the ground gives off brings to mind lilacs that have budded and blossomed. There are no more blossoms, perfume and purple gone for a year, as if forever. In heaven there are no tears, salt water wiped away entirely. One moment I breathe contentment. And then unreasoning sorrow pulses through me, an imperfect tension, as if unending. I have time on my hands. In heaven there is no more dusk, dark, dawn, meridian. And what I know now and for certain: neither the day nor the hour.

II

It seems clear enough that there is in the brain a particular pain-center, where sensations of every variety check in, to emerge as anguish and hurt. Thus there is not, as we might suppose, a multiplicity of pains, like an arsenal deployed against us, but one pain which puts on, as in a ritual theater, different masks.

It need not, even, be a great number of masks, some few faces peopling an endless repertory. From one fairy tale to another, is not the witch the same witch, whether poisoning an apple or fattening the children?

III

The doctrine changes, blows here and there, hot, cold. One more notion sweeps across the state in gusts, fiercely at first, settling then into a mild rotation. It puts things in motion. It dies down, while pressure somewhere else is building.

Called to, across a chasm of thin air, I shape the air to answer. My moments force themselves apart.

Breathe out. Breathe in. But as long as you are alive, there is a dead space in your lungs, never emptied, never needing to be filled. The spirit there, stale and sustaining, holds open every possibility, urging none. Ghost money: money to burn.

IV

On the earliest known sundial, the finger of shadow moves through symbols of the cosmos, but there are no lines drawn to mark off the hours. It does not, in the modern sense, "keep" time, but celebrates its flight, its recurrence, its brightness.

V

Hermaphrodite, sleeping. Predominance, in the visible, of the right hand — but the eyes now closed. What could there be to dream about, for one already complete? A perfect asymmetrical stability. No need to see or even to look.

To know, without having to ask. From any point on the periphery, advancing always towards the body. Both sexes. And both asleep.

VI

A scream from outside broke our argument and I ran to the door, rushed out onto the sidewalk almost, I thought, before the scream had ended. The night sky, above the street lamp, had a sheen of some dark metal.

Sirens — which seemed this evening more frequent than usual, and more strident — state the theme, you have said, of our instant: the howl of a machine hurrying to disaster. And all day, in the violence of delivery, ordinary trucks rattle our sashes.

The street lay empty, mercury lit, silence giving us no indication of which way to turn.

Easy Tales

I

Some years ago a woman of twenty married, to general astonishment, a man in his fifties who was neither well-regarded nor rich. The marriage, people said, will not last, because the woman is beautiful and will eventually come to her senses.

In less than a year, she in fact left her husband, and for a time no one knew where she had gone. When, later, she reappeared, it was with another man of roughly the same age as her husband, but a man of scabrous aspect, remembered locally for some shady but unsuccessful business dealings.

It is not known at exactly what point her husband — who at his death was still legally married to her — wrote these lines:

> *I know how old I am, now that I find*
> *It is too late to put her out of mind.*

II

Two students, boy and girl, met at a party and afterwards began to share a tiny apartment. This was in May and in June neither was willing to part, so they lived together on through July and August.

In September, they tired of each other and both found new attachments.

The following Christmas, the boy was killed in a car accident. The girl wept when she heard, and over spring vacation she wrote the following lines:

> *Could anyone, last summer, have told how*
> *We'd have nothing at all in common now?*

III

A young woman realized that her father, a widower, was going mad and would have eventually to be taken care of. Never explaining her motives to anyone, she remained single and devoted much of her time to attending him.

This became more and more difficult as years went by, one crisis following another. After a violent attack on his daughter's life, the man was committed.

The woman wrote these lines:

> *I saw my mind slip, and begin to slide,*
> *And fall-I saw it clearly, from outside.*

IV

There was a man once who, coming from a poor family, by the time he was fifty owned a substantial tract of land. His brother, however, a few years his junior, was just out of prison, where he had served a sentence for larceny.

The younger brother then came to the older, asked for a sum of money, on loan, and found himself refused.

"But I know," the younger said, "how you came by all this. No doubt you've done well, over the years, in your speculations. But your initial capital was the result of a theft."

The older did not answer, but later wrote these lines:

> *I wondered, even while we were growing, whether*
> *Fortune would ever bring us back together.*

V

A woman whose husband had died spent most of a small fortune on various attempts to contact him. She had herself never professed to believe in such practices, but her husband had, in his last illness, pleaded with such urgency that she swore to try. He then had given her a phrase which — if contact were established — he would use as proof of his identity.

During the course of innumerable failures, she became more and more nearly convinced of the possibility, and continued until she was almost without resources. At this point she received, through a medium, the following lines, which do not contain the secret phrase:

I know I felt—my love, pain, rage were real
But can't remember what it means to feel.

VI

A young man went looking for a guru. He was gone nearly fourteen months and returned just as his father was dying.

He took over his father's store, with its accumulated debts, and in two years had made it into a highly profitable business.

At this point he prepared to leave again. His mother said, "I think you are right to go. People here respect you, but they do not understand you." It was probably during a visit to his mother that he wrote these lines:

There is a mind-like place beyond the mind.
I went there, and I also stayed behind.

VII

After a fierce quarrel, ending in blows, a woman left her lover. In some days she came to him again, and a little later wrote these lines:

The rise too sharp, I swore I'd not go on,
But in the fog the path back down was gone.

The Locality Principle

Rosmarie Tells Me

of a poem I wrote to her in our early intimacy, addressing her as "Neighbor Dust," speaking of our then present state from the perspective of future decay — a future to be taken as distant.

I have no memory of this poem, but might one day write another, using, as it were, the same address.

The Man Claims

to be Ulysses, but Penelope does not believe him.

He has bent Ulysses' bow. He had slaughtered the suitors. But mere strength does not guarantee identity.

And besides, it could be a trick, a joke at her expense, the kind of joke the gods are always playing.

His old nurse recognizes a birthmark on his leg.

Penelope rejects corporeal evidence.

After all, if she were to go into that, her Ulysses was a young man — this man is old.

Only when he can tell her the pattern on the cover of the bed where they slept together their wedding night — only then, she allows that this man must be the same man, her Ulysses, whom she last saw twenty years ago.

For her, only memory insures identity.

Memory — than which nothing can be more mortal, nothing more uncertain.

Room Tone

"…how could anything other than the denial of the
body be outside time?"—— Schopenhauer

Legend

a melody runs
through my head the
notes uncertain

He breathed on them
which means (says
Augustine) He kissed them or

"in some way
placed his mouth to their mouths"

and said
receive

well or
perhaps

as one breathes
on embers

making their spirits
glow

(darkness tough
nothing
is still a barrier

and the light has never
comprehended it)

Spirit of the House

a poor thing but
my body

fear is a narrow
place un-
certain

and Orion look (they
say) there
is his belt (or
Pisces or the Great
Bear)

I do not see them

parallel lines at first
diverge then
in the distance
come together (the
stars twinkle un-
figured)

objects on the
run run more and
more slowly

the lock is broken the
page is turned the map
pre-war

and to listen
while melody

takes on particular
frequencies:
when attention is
poor the task
becomes conscious

Introduction of the Door

no direct contact
is possible

every unexpected
color

snow
cloud
mist
sea-spray

out-of-the-
mind travel

and what
world to be
considered?

time makes its
claims then
now (always when
after before un-
til)

no direct
communication

a little comma or
slightest
pause

it's not enough that
spirits merge
mountainous western

paradise or
eastern paradise
of isles

(obsessed by the opposite
of eternity)

our dust must
mingle

BODILY

my soul my ex-
ternal my
soul Ohimé

hidden

spirited away

in a bottle in
a box in a
box-car in the freight
yard over
an ocean behind the
calendar lost

(up the stairs some
dread
each
step)

in the mis-
fire of a synapse

bloody combat (earth
divided) filthy the
world of spirits
clothed in white and carrying
a ring of keys

light rending
to light

every color
unexpected

dancer in sudden
sweaty freeze

up the
stairs to our
own room

Insisting Objects

for your body or
mine

a line

(in the spill of the
lamp a
life)

I draw a
line in
the light between
infinite
and *creatures*

(the line I
drew was
like a description)

now what
is possible? and
what else?

stark branches of
leafable trees

depth at a
distance
hollows

purple for
the feel of space

(a line to
represent a line)

and in the hollow we
hesitate

Diminished Galleries

too old for
vision I must
settle for dreams

specific forms
of cloud

(body surrounded by
body)

every sensation con-
ceals a dream

fresco

figurine

sculpture in
low relief

*(a motor halo a
mental blue)*

cleft in the
logical space

(wilderness or
wrack)

we have lived
on a ladder to
the window of a
room to which
the key is lost

(words lost
in the music)

Indefinite Inscriptions

(doors strangely
opened and
strangely shut)

(rustlings like
silk)

(sometimes a
whispering and frequently
footsteps)

blue-occasioned
conduct

(coherent) world
entirely
confabulated

words
lost in their own sound

Theme

we are differently
tuned

like violin and piano

(listen)

our variations

An Entomological Souvenir

for Emmanuel Hocquard

here are the principal
transformations:

a fish
a cow
a chariot
a laurel

also:

the steps of a temple
the art of wrestling

and here the
scarab: rolling
a round of earth along

men with animal
heads with noses
bleeding

clay replicas of coins

believe me there is
no comparison

lichen:

the splendor dazzles

FEELERS

we have lived through
the world of a
preceding evening

the strongest light o-
blique is in-
visible

(except
as it spills)

time from its
lobe dis-
tributes our gestalt

the dead own
nothing not
even their tombstones

we have lived through
saints and
cannot get them
out of our names

(never actually
there to

see worm
transfigured)

(and endless hours through
the divisions of the
heart

trying to
understand that text about

dividing *soul* from
spirit)

What Could Be The Case

neighbor dust
think:

how the setting
sun advertises
autumn

how our
lightest laugh
is plummeting just as
grave things
fall

in the time it takes
time to pass I
watch our gaze
glance off

ant hills

sepia from squid or
octopus

figures from tombs

the wind *downrushing* in
headlong time

(we have hands)

here (no-
where) the intervals

are pure

and also
here

House of the Soul

vertical
memory

night
falls but day
is broken

in the mind of
natural man in the extremes
of the natural
mind:

insects

frightened I might
remember that or
this

the day
fine as any but
just about done for

(broke through fell
through dropped
down)

hearing
sorrow a slope of
sand the sound
runs down

in our own
despite

(already) having
sided with the world

and my
soul beside me

Tunnels Leading

passing through
den through nest
through burrow or
hive

dimensions
of yes and no

gigantic
birds of com-
paratively recent
times

weak river
through flowing
sand

fear in a
world
of fear

afraid all
lines
converge

what all possible
songs have in common

fear of
other
functions of memory

down to the
water bringing
nothing back

CORRIDOR

as I was
reading the
book closed like an eyelid

universe immersed
in sleep

refined to
amethyst

(you are more im-
portant to me
than words *or*
melody)

we will not remember the
word
return

The Silhouette of the Bridge

I

A disciple of the great void, still this side of Nirvana, is telling — it is a public lecture — of a man carrying a great heavy load. *Until*, one day the bottom drops out of his basket and his burden becomes light.

He — the lecturer — continues for an hour and a half in this vein, referring to enlightenment as the experience of "dropping our bottoms."

At an opera in the sometime East, during intermission, I sit down with a cup of coffee and suddenly recall sitting here before.

Here, quite certainly here, exactly at one of these tables. It is still the East. The cafe is crowded, as always during intermission, and I sit down where two other people are already having refreshments. The man, who looks as if he might head the chamber of commerce — if commerce here has chambers — seems to be trying to get acquainted with the woman. The woman is dark, a trifle hefty, maybe forty, not handsome but attractive, exotic, with an aura of power.

He asks her what she is doing in Berlin. That is an easy sentence to understand and I understand what she says in reply, because it is simple and because she speaks German slowly and with an accent.

She says she is in Berlin (I wonder where she comes from) to sing an opera. She will sing — in another house — Madama Butterfly. The man looks blank.

"Do you know," she asks slowly, with an accent, *"Madama Butterfly?"*

He shakes his head absently. No, he does not.

Light spills.

I come to Providence at the age Dante stumbles into Hell.

At age eight, or maybe ten, I keep a diary — nothing extensive, more, as I remember, of events than of feelings.

After a few weeks, I discover that my father — I don't at first believe it — simply sits down and opens and reads my diary.

I throw it away.

I never keep another.

So many believe, through so many centuries, that we are each a little universe, a small glass mirroring the whole shebang, which is represented in us tiny but complete, a microcosm.

Avicenna has a different take on this. We are, he supposes, nothing in ourselves — nothing, that is, to start with. But we can, by thought, gradually, take in the macrocosm, reflecting all things, thing by thing, until we *become* a little mirror of the Whole. Indeed, if we fail to do so, our souls go into eternity maimed, partial.

A singer's death is more affecting than that of a writer, since a poem or a story stands at more of a distance from the body that has produced it.

I go into the front hall to lock the door for the night.

Minutes later, I ask myself if I have locked the door. I cannot remember the actual locking, cannot feel in my fingers the turn of the latch, the echo of fixing the chain.

I go back to the front hall, find the door latched, the chain fixed.

Curious, how Simone Weil makes into opposites *gravity* and *grace*, while Augustine knows his love of God as a load or heavy weight, a kind of ballast.

To be home, I must live where I remember living.

The number of sparrows increases. And pigeons. Gangs of blue-jays.

The rarer birds all but disappear.

I am not, in Providence, quite at home — though it has been my home longer than anywhere else.

I am offered, with coffee, a madeleine. The only recollection it provokes is of reading Proust.

I have not acquired the dialect: brooks are still creeks to me.

Someone says "the past" is not something that happens, but a scenario in my head, thus making me responsible.

Avicenna dies of (unspecified) sexual excesses.

This, now, is a kind of diary-in-memory, posthumous to what is recorded, inscriptions above buried impressions.

I know, of course, that while memory holds the shape of the past, the past that is held takes on the shape of memory.

Our eye scapes the land.

A song is determined by the nature and training of the voice.

Our space is a vase, the objects within it like water taking the vase's shape.

A "haunting, ineluctable sense of cosmic memory" may derive from "the evening darkness on the rear platform of an Elmgrove Ave. car."

This play of memory, now, is my *bel canto*.

I do not remember that evening's darkness.

Or the platform.

There is no Elmgrove car.

I remember *chalcedony*. And, thereby, the New Jerusalem.

…unique among American cities in having, for its local color, horror stories.

Music for a while…

Less and less.

And that terrible cherry pie…

And how it ends, how will I know? Crashing the threshold of knowing, I am suddenly past it, cancelling even the awareness of crossing, cancelling it retroactively and irrevocably. That is to say, I may feel the shock at the instant of shock, but at that very instant lose it again.

And if ever I reawaken, which is unimaginable, I will still not remember.

I do not think such momentary feeling can be called experience.

memory palace in
decay but

before the final
darkening

(just what *did* I mean by "bridge")

goes through a
stage in which past
images still
stand at stations but

odd sequence at
strange angles jutting

(sometimes broken perspectives)

perplexed by figures as
familiar as hands but

now a plain, now
a public path

in a botched
gestalt

(upheaval)

*

I am not tired. And yet, like a column, sleep invades me.

*

In the heat of the day, and the year, I walk to the corner where snow, swirled by a chill wind, breaks the light from the streetlamp into brilliant flurries between me and the dark empty sky.

I have sought a truce with time.

I am not just any
event my
cause is in

question I am
highly unexpected

in the case of bodies
moving my
body could move forever

(my imagined body
along its natural
path)

suppose for example out
the window
along a tangent to

its orbit this
pattern follows

*

Since my tooth, as my dentist has decreed, must out, I make an appointment and deliver myself to the office on Waterman Street.

      "This is not tooth extraction," says the receptionist. "It is oral surgery."

The difference seems to be in dollars.

A student takes my blood pressure. I know she is a student, because the surgeon — once I am in his chair — explains every move he makes. Not to me, but to her.

She is attentive.

"You see," he says. "Second lower left biscuspid." He is, meanwhile, injecting. He has a high, squeaky voice. "Soon he won't feel a thing."

And, soon, I don't feel a thing.

"We'll try," he tells her, "just to pull it. But" — where have I heard this before? — "probably it will explode."

Which, I gather, it does. But my attention is elsewhere, fixed by then entirely on her eyes. Which are close to mine. From which proceed rays of almost visible intellect. Cold fire. Her gaze never wanders up to *my* fascinated eyes, never, I'm sure, takes any impression of my face.

I listen to exalted strains, while you are watching for indications. The air is heavy, streets damp from no noticeable rain.

At noon (which is to say, suddenly) the house seems full of people: people napping, chatting, guests at a sacrifice, tourists on an exhausting excursion.

She attends, without wavering, to the cavern of my mouth, missing no maneuver of her master's art.

In the first room: a body clothed, armed, ornamented.

In the second: simple radiance, warm objects and the cold invisible.

He is chipping out broken root, digging (while describing) ivory shrapnel.

Peter went raving mad before he died, having the satisfaction at last (at least) of out-suffering (albeit for a shorter space of time) his model *the* Crucified.

And in the third room: much care, silliness, much melancholy.

You shall have no food to eat. On city streets, in ruins, dark corners of the house.

Perpetual terror and howl of the stormwind. No wings. No winged helmet. No shoes with wings. You shall have no water from the bloody river.

Your past is obsolete. Ambush is your alternative.

Her eyes seem not to blink, so intent are they on technique.

The fourth room. Here is St Luke, physician, drawing the Virgin. Here a plethora of prophetic superscriptions. Wick lamps of Lascaux. Flush toilets in Mohenjodaro.

In rooms to follow, not more concern than crossing an avenue. Abstruse omens.

Crocodile when least expected.

The gum is sewn. Mouth allowed to close on its wound. Her eyes withdraw, no longer interested.

*

And He ascended — the Christ — ascended "on high."

But just where did He go? And by what route? (For while there is no controversy about His upward motion while within sight of the apostles, there *is* disagreement about his itinerary afterwards.)

Well, never mind. He went, in any case — as Saint Thomas says somewhere — beyond anything that could properly be called locality.

*

Jeanne Longyear comes across a convent church in Brittany, or maybe Normandy. Parts of the building are undergoing restoration and there is unsightly scaffolding, outside and in.

Against a temporary partition, blocking off one chapel, a ladder is leaning. Jeanne thinks if she climbs this ladder, she will be able to see into the chapel.

She climbs.

She climbs farther, to see what she can see.

As her head surmounts the obstacle, what she sees is a group of nuns, just now distracted from their devotions by the startling apparition, above the altar, of Jeanne's startled face.

Jeanne descends quickly.

Quickly she leaves the church.

No report of a vision is recorded.

*

Hannah calls to communicate an outrage. Her dentist — he has been her dentist since she was a child — has thrown her out of his dentist's chair.

She goes on about it.

"Hannah," I put in, "why? What did you do to him?"

"Oh," she says, "nothing... that is... well... I bit his hand."

*

My brother Charles squats in a condemned building. His living quarter runs with mice, but in an abandoned garage across the alley, he collects stray rats — with whom he obviously identifies.

"You see," he says, petting one of his guests as he puts out their food, "if they're taken care of and *don't have to make a living*, they're peaceable, friendly, cause no problems."

*

I throw trash behind a mirror.

*

I have heard (but is it true?) that if one has rats, one can be sure (small consolation, it might seem) that one will not have — in the same area — mice.

*

Then too, I used to know a philosopher, who seemed to believe that mice were baby rats.

*

no definition (in the
commentary) but he *is*
already in the world
the restored
Nero he will
sit in the Temple and

give himself out for God
but be
slain at the
Second Coming

...told them
all this but
will not tell us

the devil is
downpour winds
are wicked spirits with
a motion a-
gainst the saints

he will reveal (later, in
a part of the commentary now
lost) the
vertiginous
rivers of anti-Christ

*

Between New York and Providence, on Amtrak's rusty rails, I am not
the only person in the coach, but there are few travelers tonight and I
may well be the only one awake.

I look up from my book, because I *know* I will see someone coming
into the car — and I do — and I know also that the figure just entering (the
train is clicking along, it is not a station) is about to disappear.

It is not something I can explain.

Nothing distinguishes her — it is a woman — from just
another passenger coming from the vestibule. I see her distinctly. That
is to say, she is not shadowy or transparent. She wears a simple light
coat, a hat like a rain-hat. I do not see her face, though at less than half
a car's length I suppose I should. I do not know how I know she is Asian

or, for that matter, what makes me certain it is a woman.

But there is not much time and, for what little there is, I am *convinced* that she will not, coming down the aisle, get to where I am sitting, because — I have no doubt — there is no one there.

And, sure enough, she vanishes, not sinking out of sight, not fading away. Simply, she's gone.

No fear, no joy, accompanies this apparition. For all I can tell, nothing is predicted, nothing commemorated.

*

inside un-
comfortable

any way
out
uneasy

*

I had not realized how dark it is, inside the body.

*

An uncertain path we walk, the line — ill-marked and slippery — between inhibition and exhibition.

I wake, tired of sleep and terrorized by its intimations.

Knights give up their way of life, move into town and take up trades to sustain themselves and their families.

I wake, unsure where I am, I and my surroundings vague, the fierce sense of reality having disappeared with the dream.

Semiramis if I Remember

thoughts among the un-
thought — hair
and breasts

individual syllables, be-
yond the body

sleepless

my description
profane, likewise my
understanding

foul and pure like
any idea

to manipulate
winds, dream
and no dream

or fire

or water

smoke, a
lamp or

fireflies

an appearance like
cloudless

sky

junction
of day and night, dreamless

dreaming

*

I am the virgin Mary.
I am Switzerland.
This is a terrible coincidence.

I'm the Emperor of China.
I cannot stand emptiness.
I talk on stilts.

I twist per minute.
I stand where the dial stands.
I allow for current.

I walk on the radio.
I will rattle you to tears.
You are fortunate not to know me.

I kill anything but time.

*

I write a poem and title it *"SEAS" NOT SEAS*, and that title seems right.

Until I hear myself saying, *Seize Nazis.*

As when, adolescent, I was scornful of the hymn books that had corrupted a text.

Prayer is the soul's sincere desire,
                 Uttered or unexpressed...

the poet had written. But we were singing,

Prayer is the soul's sincere desire,
                 Unuttered or expressed...

The meaning, I had to admit, was unchanged — which made the revision seem all the more gratuitous. My pedantry was provoked and the next time that hymn came around, I trumpeted out, to the usual tune, the original words.

And heard, with a shock, my own voice, too late to call back, on its own,

                 Prayer is the soul's sincere desire,
                 A turd or unexpressed...

             *

from lack of sleep
delirium, pillar of
fire by night

perpetual light from a
western lamp, a single
lamp pretending to keep
God awake

eternal His
Sabbath, His seventh day
unending

the eighth
day
ours

FROM ANALOGIES OF ESCAPE

1997

STANDARD CANDLES

I
this house my
house is not
always here and some-
times I feel like a

different person

What was I thinking of?

II
noon and the
brink of death and I
roll in the snow, depending
on the weather

Let us assume the saints had something besides gravity.

III
what cannot be
handled what
cannot be imagined
shoeing for a walk to

Jerusalem

waiting for our friends and our
bodies very
old and distant
objects weaker on

mountaintops
stronger at the
poles the stranger
strange
unrising

body

Tow shadows lock.

IV
every part
weeping even the
bird the bubble the prison
a sphere with eyes before and

behind

foreign country

Angels know no particulars.

Waiting is a form of violence.

V
This is the house I did not build.

This is the room at the top of the stairs in a house I didn't build.

This is the desk — from a different generation — wedged in the window-nook of an upstairs room in a house someone else built.

This is the mess I've made. Under it all is a fire I did not set.

In the noise the world makes there is no window and here I lay my words in the *loud*, in the *burning*, the *built*. This is a fire from before ever fire came down.

This is my mess, over the noise of fire, window, desk, stair, house.

VI
trumpets and
banners trumpets
and cymbals bowls
brimming

Enoch and Elijah at
the end of time

personalities
rarely connected with well-
formulated thoughts

POET

The wind dying, I find a city deserted, except for crowds of people moving and standing.

Those standing resemble stories, like stones, coal from the death of plants, bricks in the shape of teeth.

I begin now to write down all the places I have not been —starting with the most distant.

I build houses that I will not inhabit.

Trains

In a harsh light, shadowless, I dream of trains.

   Unconcealed, without the doubt of a shadow, I dream a life filled with roulade and with vocalise, the elements at large coupled by vanity.

*

Now I begin to paint shadows in.

from DOCTOR TRANSOM, NOTES FOR A MEMOIR

"Those who roar most loudly rarely sing in time."
Caruso

Introducing Doctor Transom

his way of walking
irretrievably
lost along with
shoes of a particular fashion

he has inadvertent
virtues many and
strange diseases many and strange
delights

warmth and will and
texture — he
believes in the bloody and depends
on angels

the river *floweth* so says
his oracle I am not
obliged to
believe it

a remark which may be applied to his
whole history — phenomena
of rivers
rain in small and larger drops

Doctor Transom to Nurse Fanlight
[Possible Song]

the final impression
who can tell
who can imagine
the freeing of a single cell

a counterpoison
junk DNA
who can predict
the ending of imperfect day

you know I'd love you if I could
you know that nothing's
hidden or misunderstood

the roof is falling

                    *

down in the heart of it
what's the trick
no one supposes the judge to be just
and *am I not sick?*

steps of the intellect
a slippery-slide
which of us can even guess
what's doing on the other side

not the word I meant to say
though to be quite frank
I waited all day

I live before your time

*

thought past thinking
concepts blind
why not be reconciled
to a millenium passing out of mind

I know I'll never be at ease
till the textbook
brings me my disease

does passive resistance prove free will?

Doctor Transom,
Some of his Delights

let us he
suggests walk in
groves and gardens
grottoes fairgrounds

transparent lakes delicious
scenery
scent
sound

wisdom is he
says in thes
perilous days
to attack

from the abdomen
depression he claims is
on the rise hence he
hums "Qui sdegno" (from

The Magic Flute)
or
"Love Me
and the World Is Mine"

ANALOGIES OF ESCAPE

Doctor Transom Examines the Singer

ah the word *ah*
I see you have a
naturally placed
voice its delicate

lining never
tripping over
tessitura now
always attack

with indifference
the arrangement the mouth
makes getting ready to
smile

poison
with the charm of
intonation don't
ever desire contraries...

— *a little wider...*

...now go
practice with your
mouth closed
when it is

closed
the voice finds
other channels some
preponderance

of mind, so
partial as
to be practically
negative

Nurse Fanlight to Doctor Transom
[Possible Song]

from scratch
to scratched
blessing and curse
confusion of the knees
worse and worse

from darker
to dark
doctor and nurse
dewdrops begin to freeze
worse and worse

unattached
shadows
pocket and purse
between the sky and the subway station
worse and worse

a grasp
of the fact
prolix and terse
to wilt at its ease
worse and worse

eyes covered
eyes alert
emerge immerse
run after revelation
worse and worse

wait let me
see you wait
chapter and verse
yesterday's joy embarrasses
worse and worse

big bang
to final crunch
forceps and hearse
cloudy cloud-terraces
worse
and worse

SENSATION

evening prayer: the upper line
is surface soul, the lower sub-
stratum rocky

simply go there is no
limit

hence the beginning of
this narrative

inevitable

keen
edge — sharp enough
to be

recognized by the brain

FROM HAUNT

2000

Potential Random

for Barbara Guest

"…in deep sleep, the mind may come closest to perfecting rational thought. We have no reason for asserting the opposite, except that when we wake we do not remember our idea."

Immanuel Kant

Potential Random I

alight
settle down
make a stop
linger

the alighting of birds

through a place
pass
dance wandering women
rebel
(unstable)

pinched off from a piece of clay

a kind of earth or soil
weakness
rejection

asphalt in the third millenium

unconscious recipient of mercy

caulking for Noah's ark
the basket in which Moses was placed
and the Nile
dependent on water
solemn
set up camp

(watch me disappear)
unafraid

filled with terror

fat
shelter
rest
be quiet

Potential Random II

Many books have been destroyed, carelessly or by design. Lost, burnt, forgotten, volumes drop out of existence, along with — more easily disposed of — proofs never pulled, unpublished manuscripts, notes for books, plans and proposals for things to be written, collected, put into books. The number of projects unaccomplished in history must be enormous.

And much larger, almost infinite, the realm of projects unattempted, never started, what no one ever thought to try.

My doctrine would derive, not from wisdom concealed by anxious arhats in caves beneath impassable Himalayas, nor from a chain of unwritten instruction passed guru-wise down centuries. It would remain in a world beneath notice, too obvious to be considered. Thus, secret.

The world as it lies open here, waiting for me to fail.

I do not need to know your real name.

This much seems obvious, that as we move along the path, slowly but certainly the path replaces us. And also, just as strands in the vitreous humour cloud the visual field, words stray, making our thought opaque.

Potential Random III

Ship is in danger, ship
must be repaired, but ship must
continue afloat as long as we continue
crossing the dangerous waters.

These events take place in order that they may be represented.

Egypt is memory, captivity in Egypt
is memory. Ship of the
North with its
anchor from the South, it rides above the Ur-Fish.

From many names for God come
many gods. If you believe in any,
you may know how the body could be glorified.

And if you will rise with that
withered arm…

Names of things
can never enter Heaven.

Turn now, together with your body — turn
past the five windows, past
your pride in the dark image and your
body turning.

Waking, doomsday for some dream.

Words perish, like the word for oyster. Words
are a great retreat — they are
like strips of existing or like
sea-shells echoing words.

POTENTIAL RANDOM IV

A view of the landscape.

up

A view of the river, of
bathers along the bank.

down

Now a view of the view, a
sheer perspective.

charmed

He is sent away, so
begins to exist.

strange

Homeward bound taxi: rather hazy idea.

top (or truth)

Surely he'll find something to
say on the silliness of opera.

bottom (or beauty)

Stand here, where without too great a turn, my eyes meet your eyes mirrored. And my eyes in the mirror, your eyes.

Whatever's to either side of us runs out of the frame and is lost. What's behind us is lost behind us.

Reduced to picture, we can appreciate our picture, reversed but right side up. Our lines of sight are straightforward — the surface glassy, clear.

Simple and astonishing, the location of bodies, grandly irregular in the smooth surrounding echo.

Potential Random VI

wicked at first
tore their clothes
refusing to speak
took off their sandals

I know not what

fasted
ready by tomorrow
gashed themselves
exactly at midnight
freely lamented

I know not whither

wept

Potential Random VII

What is seen then, as the center, is not the center, but only light feeding into the center.

Devastation, ritual of covenant accompanied by darkness.

Wash your clothes.

Shave off your hair.

Bathe yourself in water.

All space becomes neutral.

Uncaulked and unprovisioned, we reach shore.

Something must be done about darkness before we can live in this light.

Cold air and warm air twinkle the starlight, Nobody's mother tongue.

Potential Random VIII

At the mouth of the stream, there is a mysterious island.
A mountain on the island.
The trees there bear (no Tree-of-Life) precious stones.
A place of desires.

I crouch down in my torn clothes.
Bloodstained cloak.
I cut off my hair and howl.
Slain man wallowing in his blood.

They are so terrified they forget to call for mourners.
The other side of death.
They mourn with astonishing frequency.
A razor from beyond the Euphrates.

She saunters under quick green trees, angels falling around her.
Chinks in the rational.
Song turns into lamentation.
Canopy of darkness.

Soldiers offer strawberry coral.
Eidola.
The dark is slippery.
Shapeless logs, sacred stones, then images.

Potential Random IX

The shapes of things rise up against me — cube, pyramid, cone —
actual, ideal — and threaten to trip me up, obstruct me, box me in.

They lie in wait. They spring from my own eyes.

I take them all, straight-lined or curved, reducing each to a circle —
closed, each circle, by a movement of my hand.

Potential Random X

No counting the
number of the dead, the number
of those who will die.

Kant thought Earth had at one time, like Saturn, a ring. Composed of
watery vapors, it encircled the world in beauty, to be regarded and
appreciated by Earth's inhabitants.

In the course of time, from the action of a comet or other
cause, the waters composing that ring were loosed and fell upon Earth
and in that deluge the greater part of a sinful mankind perished.

Lost thereby, for the survivors, which is to say, for us: the
sight of that ring in the upper air, the most exquisite view from the
surface of Paradise or a young planet — our rainbow a faint reminder
of the glory lost.

At the center of every
system is a flaming
body.

Bright sun between
grapevine and fig tree.

By coincidence,
sun and moon
are exactly the same size.

Celestial phenomena — there are
so many stars — merge along
my line of sight.

Directly before my eye descends

a spider — slowly, a ways
away, just down to eye-level.

Earth spins in the
sun's corona.

High countries in the
dust, and also
elephants, alas.

A hundred miles of
umbra over un-
counted acres of tundra.

I try to find some
sense in which behind is
not in back of.

It suggests the
idea of a bird.

Monstrous colors on
certain things.

Monstrous things in
uncertain colors.

One has to choose between
life
and what life contains.

Sunspots freeze in place.

Traveling some current, the
road imponderable.

Wastrel and hangman

thrive in the conquered
city.

What have I ever wanted to
say, but
how at this moment

He walks in darkness, sits in darkness, dwells. Darkness falls, clouds, covers.

Or clouds of insects.

Or extinguishing a lamp.

After so many years, it ought to be infinite, but it never is and car lights glide so easily across his ceiling.

Neither cornlands, nor well-kept vineyards, only...

He cannot decide whether it's better to regard the soul as asleep or to take what seems like dream to be the waking world.

Scattered objects must have something to tell. Between the stars, between the positive particles, there is said to be "nothing" — can he hold this?

Delicate arms, bare, a hopeless gesture.

He cannot decide if cosmic fire creates the universe or ignites as executioner. The bitten line is broken, resembling lightning in a mediocre sky.

He cannot decide whether it is a friend in a dream speaking to him of danger, or a dangerous dream instructing him to act for the sake of the hypnotist.

His face darkens, with the darkness of delight.

He dreams a costume dream. What colors are latent in his darkness?

He does know that there are other shadows — uncertainties, headlights, fires on the beach at Nice, the horror of being chosen.

At moments life is so transparent that everything seems real, seems anyway familiar, distantly, like the aging face of someone he last saw young.

He cannot tell if his dream — so quickly forgotten — roused this storm in his soul, or if anxiety springs from his being awake, alert, dreamless.

…sallow throng beside dismal pool…

A very high and concave roof. He cannot decide where reason ends, associating as he does darkness with creation.

Between now and now, was time — will time be — empty?

What runs in the dark, or in daylight from stone to stone, sudden as spasm, a streak of blood?

Sheer throb relaxes into the mirror opposite, hard to follow, complex but quite complete. Losing certain colors might impoverish his visual life, but he realizes that a flaw in the numerical system would weaken the structure of the world.

With sunrise comes battle.

How is it, sensitive to signs of the times, he finds it so hard to decipher headlines?

And in what body would he like to be raised?

He is no more present to himself than objects in his view — the journey, long for so short a life, promising agate, chalcedony. He attends to changing expression, flickers of shadow, to keep his thought from running inward to inward light.

HAUNT

He cannot decide whether to change the subject.

He sings English and understands it is not always possible to make clear distinctions.

Sees no cause, he, to do no otherwise.

He considers movement, perhaps in the sense of change, honing the sword.

He cannot decide whether to describe his death in terms of hunger and sundown — or like a new-born babe, in the course of its disaster.

There have been some more overwhelmed than he with shame, with pity and terror — the east ablaze, the city's spires afire.

He cannot decide if the experiment is local, all life composed on this periphery, or if along the wall of stars there's by chance another creature — farther than faintest signals — signifying.

Potential Random XII

Now a warm wind riffles
the leaves, ransacks the neighborhood.

You will not wake up for me.

In a certain chord, by the western loop of
Ermine Street, tomorrow
is well known, speckling as it does
flagstone and flag, slim white hands.

The street ripples, roars. Take
it all away, lay it among
the scarcely remembered.

As we stroll, a thick crust
underfoot and perfectly firm, beautiful
eyes and
teeth flashing.

Moss may
edge the brook, tree-shaded
streets sleep, shadow-damaged, under
a late sun.

Snakes hate summer and are
revived by rain.

Housetops glitter a long-forgotten
flame, a frightful dream. But do not
ever dream of ghosts: they will undo
your remembering.

Lateen shades, lace curtains, rich
tumuli, the stillest city
swarms with hurry.

Our restless fingers, so they
stand. Throbbing
silence, darkening room.

Irrelevant, my own attire blood-
stained and ragged, what
nightmare sleeping or
awake, prying the bolted scuttle.

Otherwise, no signal for fear.

No sea-sickness in heaven.

Reality, Aristotle says, is not
a daytime serial.

Then comes Love's
army, disemboweled, Love's own
cavalry, guts
hanging from the saddle.

Adventures on my pillow and
below the snow-line.

A fierce pride
blazes at any
hint of earthly pleasure.

POTENTIAL RANDOM XIII

tall grain
food for the dead

a contest with uncleanness
detestable things

desire

thought

wallow in ashes
wail aloud
howl
scream

covering cherub

ideas of death

POTENTIAL RANDOM XIV

An aging house, well yes he
understands that — but suddenly
down it falls.

And he is in a garden.

And there are animals.

And he is in a garden and
there are trees.

And there are stones on
fire.

And, well, he walks
up and down on them.

But this is
the Hebrew *and*, not
a conjunction, merely some un-
translatable particle.

Cenotaph (there is no
body here).

(Somehow I can't imagine
digging a separate grave for the heart.)

And everything is cast
down — plants, animals,
garden, stones, fire, Tyre
with its river called
Litany — along with himself.

The living organism, he
hears, is a
symbol of the psyche.

Thinking is inward seeing.
So Wittgenstein thought, and also
Swedenborg.

Die, well yes he knows he
has to, but thinks of it as being
killed — or killing.

As if at a distance — he
lives, not in
life, but across from it.

And it comes to pass.

And he tries to distinguish
life and its contents.

And they wheel around him, the cars, as
if he were standing still.

POTENTIAL RANDOM XV

Three lists remain: The first
is a list of the living,

who are now dead. The second records
the saints and martyrs, those

who laid down their lives to
be with Jesus. They fly to Him,

to miss the long repose.
The third list

is a list of the dead.

POTENTIAL RANDOM XVI

The days fan out, free and fragmentary, leaving him night — night folded around him and also inevitable unfolding night.

He is not absolutely sure the heavenly bodies are capable of desire.

Low decorative screens that he adores for their design conceal household gods and other holy objects.

He thinks of Moses, prepared to slay the death-angel.

Or Pisgah.

Love, in its mountain ranges.

Transhuman.

In earlier travels, he saw red windblown sand.

He has been told that the number of stars in the sky, whatever it is, is just the right number.

Also, that before he goes away again, he should file a change of address. There is no bravery more stubborn than this: the dead lie where they fall.

But note, he does not tell us, or even himself, everything. And, besides, this world lasts only so long as it lacks balance — the veer preserves us.

Passing regiments, glittering steel, outcurving flame, incoherent pollen. Note also, this poem is quite impersonal.

Hints reach him that stars of an earlier generation, crumbled to dust, haunt all the corridors.

Loath to part from his early life — or its aftertaste — trailing thus through nothing to nothing.

Cascades of unbound hair.
Ineffable cushions.

He can never manage to distinguish death's three weapons: a song, a dance, and whatever is absolutely pointless.

Hills surround abscissa, ordinate, simplest functions, the light too strong for more intricate patterns.

And among these secular representations, uncomfortable laughter.

In the shadow of the house, the tree. Then distant shots, a hollow roar. Traditional bonfires blaze on hilltops. Wrecked cafes across rainfilled streets. Glass-littered sidewalks.

This room, this door, this valley open on all sides, quick with the terror of choosing.

...eyeless sockets...

...fire-ravaged hair...

He cannot keep in mind how any thought left to itself, any autonomous act of the brain, is terrible — destruction if awake — asleep, a revelation — or even how the ligature of bones runs fast as lightning in the night.

His dream no longer upsets him — outlying barrows, cold, clustered, as if there really were a god of the cold — until he notices it is in color.

He cannot decide whether to wish for day or to wish for a day's return or to wish for a decision.

The last moment, here, now, reflected, sliding to its fade —
he looks forward to it, such as it was.

He has been spared, on more than one occasion, unreasonable
happiness.

Potential Random XVII

augury
witchcraft
blob-like clouds
a pagan or a foreign hairstyle

I adapt this to the apprehension of humankind.

a circle or something that can be rolled
light-years from the center
round
inner rim of the disc of clouds
wheel
heavily processed inside stars
the wheel of a chariot
the central cluster
a round thistle
five billion years
wheel at the cistern

And also to the understanding of angels.

tightly packed stars
dwelling place of demons
dust warmed by the stars
haunt of jackals
the surrounding gas
without inhabitant

Tuning

Herr Stimmung — purblind — moves in corporeal time.

Think how many, by now, have escaped the world's memory.

Think, how all his wandering is only thought. Having once tried to live in the quasi-stupor of sensation, now he picks his way through areas of spilth, seeking the least among infinite evils.

His hope: intermittent.

To a person so little conscious, what would it mean to die? Though he feels, true enough, death's wither-clench. Thinking always of something permanent, watching the while how everything goes on changing.

He has seen where Speed is buried. Eyes exorbitant.

He has the tension of male and female: active, divided. Anger and lust. What he eats tastes exactly like real food.

He would search out interphenomena, if he could decipher the interstices. The broken line. Immediate havoc. Circular heaven. Square earth. He cries world world, and there is no world.

He claims superiority over the other animals, being the only one who can talk, the only one to have doubts.

Herr Stimmung knows a whale is big. Its skeleton might shelter a dozen men.

Not existing, not subsisting — *in*sisting. Not object, not subject — *e*ject. (He works within opposed systems, every one of them opposed to system.)

"Fillette" — in confusion he addresses himself — "n'allez pas au bois seulette."

He knows who is allowed to wear what kinds of beads. He knows how fruit trees are inherited. All his self-objects lie in the inoperative past.

Herr Stimmung springs from a long undocumented ancestry.

He has a special attitude towards terror.

What Herr Stimmung Admires

The famous harp-playing donkey at Aulnay.

Figure-eight fiddles.

Percussion at funerals.

The soul-bird Ba.

The cheek-teeth of the Least Weasel.

Melusine — with wings and a fish tail, "*but does not play an instrument*."

All dancing in cemeteries.

Any dancing-all-night.

Avicenna's treatment for love sickness: old woman mimicking the appearance of the beloved (shameful parody).

Spinoza's evidence for angels' flight.

Fallacious pathos.

Rolling hard-boiled eggs downhill.

Herr Stimmung Has Doubts

He finds the claim (whom is he reading: Hegel? Brentano?) that Matter [i.e., "presentation"] is possible independently.

Whereas Quality [e.g., desire for...] is dependent on being linked to a presentation.

This makes sense.

But is it the case?

Desire without object, fear without object, love without object, seem to him not uncommon.

He begins to doubt, rather, that any object can enter our field on its own, without summons.

Summoned by a "Quality":

Desire...

Dread...

Guilt...

And as if all his thinking were merely a slide in this direction, he feels the presentation fail, making each moment of fulfillment a mountain of frustration.

Herr Stimmung on Transparency

To those of a certain temperament, there is nothing worse than the thought of something hidden, secret, withheld from their knowing — especially if they suspect that another knows about it and has even, perhaps, connived at keeping it concealed.

D.H. Lawrence seems to have been irritated no end by the thought that people were having sex and not telling him.

Freud too.

— Ah but then Freud arranged it so that everyone had to tell.

His psychoanalysis lights up the depths, makes our tangled web transparent, to the point where *I* can see all the way down to *It*.

And the process moves outward in increasing rings:

The Master analyses his disciples. Who thereby — transparent now — become masters and, in turn, take on others, patients or disciples, to analyse.

So that eventually there are no secrets.

Except, of course, those of the first Master, the Self-Analysed.

Which is to say, the only private One, sole Unrevealed. Opaque center of His universal panopticon.

While we see only His words, His daughter, His cigar.

Poor Lawrence.

The Harpies

Incessant song!

The harpies do not kill their victims...

If we could only have, while awaiting the soul, a history of heavenly music!

...nor do they transport their victims to Hades.

(The lute belongs to Venus.)

They carry their victims merely out of mind, out of remembered events, out of the world's long-term memory. Rough melody, squawk of extinction, unnoticed.

The Palmer-Worm

and even lovers talk
sometimes of other things

like

*

pain

slips into songs

divines the light

*

talks in one
voice, sings
in another

*

blind fire

*

forgetfulness and
the wand

deflect the
voice from its
customary range

*

and some words

like

*

…and after the evening and
the morning, the same
blindness

*

no rest while we
know we have to go

no place if

like

*

desire for the body as
if for the dead
body

The Higher Spin

Ararat lies
askew, along with

other beliefs, other
madnesses

a candle in a
dead man's hand

bad cess
to Orpheus and likewise to
Lot's wife

in our front
yard, protecting
us, the holly

but who knows what
love is love enough

unlucky for
sure to say
goodnight more than
once

artificial, all my
exegeses

and like God, who finished neither
earth nor heaven, I leave
all my projects
infinite

creep under
the thorn

Mirror

dark spaces

*

echoes: I will
outremember you…

*

the hollow, drumlike
sound one hears while
walking on shell ice

*

mirror effects: a rival
throne in the north

*

planets, fixed in
elliptical orbits, the stars
"in their courses"

*

repercussions: Occam's
razor or any
old saw

*

we meet
and then we
meet by chance

Paradise

in this garden every
leaf is
mortal

every petal

root and branch
grow towards
nothing

the path we
follow disappears
behind us

dreams unable to
survive the night

flowers
shed their meanings

the code that numbers the
colors of the flowers
will die

and numbers are mortal

. . . .

I wish I could
tell you
this

On Earth

this is the original
theme, through the
manifold in-
variant

rests on my
hand all
indication

*

and note how the face
disappears into the
eyes

SHIFTERS

birds I hear
weeping
and certain carhorns
seem to call my name

the sound comes
down and
inward, honk
weeping
song

not words but
wing-sounds

there is no *nothing*

GRAVITY

disappearing, you
complete the night

FROM:

SONGS FROM THE DECLINE OF THE WEST
1970

NO: A JOURNAL OF THE ARTS
2003

THE WIND IS LAUGHING

My love and I sat down to lunch,
And while I was tucking my bib
I heard time's teeth come together crunch
And I felt a sharp pain in my rib.

And I thought how the years get short while days get longer
And how old men get weak, old women stronger,
And the wind I feel now feels nice to me,
But later the same wind will blow right through me,
And the wind is laughing.

My love and I sat down to dinner,
And while I was fanning my soup
My love said my hair was looking thinner
And I felt my shoulders beginning to stoop.

And I thought how although it's likely I'll still adore her
The safest bet is always to bet on horror,
And the wind I feel now feels nice to me,
But later the same wind will blow right through me,
And the wind is laughing.

My love and I got up for breakfast,
And while I was gulping my yolk
My love, whose laugh is as quick as the quickest,
Laughed, and we laughed till I thought I would choke.

And I know the air is poison and no waters healing
And years are going to blow by forever without feeling,
But the wind we feel now feels nice to us,
And later the same wind will blow right through us,
But the wind is laughing.

A Turning Point

I come to you from crowded places,
I come to you with senses overgrown,
I come to you from a great blur of faces,
I come to you to find myself my own.

You are the stop my mind makes between losses,
You are the images I do not need to keep,
You are my wakefulness that turns and tosses,
You are the movement of my eyes in sleep.

And you improvise my meditations,
And you open up my view,
And you direct me through the streets and stations,
And you maintain the space through which I come to you.

You are the stop my mind makes between losses,
You are the images I do not need to keep,
You are my wakefulness that turns and tosses,
You are the movement of my eyes in sleep.

THE STILL OF THE NIGHT

[after Kurt Tucholsky]

In the still of the night, in bed with your only wife,
You try and figure out what it is that's missing in your life.
You're all on edge. You think, If only I had
Whatever it is I don't have, things wouldn't be this bad.
You turn and toss and think of all
You'll change tomorrow. Tomorrow, we'll see....
It's always we want someone statuesque and tall,
And we get somebody short, fat —
C'est la vie.

Every day you read the news and fall into the old rage:
Your fury reaches new heights as you read on down the page.
You feel you're wasted among all the wasted lives
In this thickly settled region with its danger of hidden drives.
Surely there was some point when you missed a call.
The expedition left while you were reaching for your clothes....
It's always we want someone statuesque and tall,
And we get somebody short, fat —
So it goes.

In the still of the night, the future seems behind.
Your prospects are so dim they're hard to bring to mind.
You've loads of plans — and some notion what they're worth:
God had a great idea, but what he came up with was the earth.
We try to stay active, we end up in fidgets.
We want a righteous leader and we get one who's religious....
It's always we want someone statuesque and tall,
And we get somebody short, fat —

Song for Crossing a Bridge

This song started with Eve, my mother,
Who lived in an orchard at one end of the world.
She was offered an apple but she bit into another,
And, ordered out, these were the words she hurled:

Well, shit, we couldn't hold on to it,
It's out the old conduit,
Down the river
Into the open sea.

A king once died, sitting on the pot,
Watching in his mind's eye his kingdom grow,
And trying to keep a finger on everything he'd ever got —
The core of the problem is letting it go,

Since, shit, you just can't hold on to it,
It's out the old conduit,
Down the river
Into the open sea.

There's something nice about living while an age is ending
And another is doing its best to be born.
Neither the old nor the new is worth defending —
The flesh on the fruit is there to be torn

Because, shit, nobody can hold on to it,
It's out the old conduit,
Down the river
Into the open sea.

LESSONING

I never learned a thing from you,
At least not anything that would do.
All that nothing in your face —
You never taught me, because you never knew
Everything comes back again, but
Not to the same place.

I bet the world that I was right.
The terms don't seem as clear tonight.
All that nothing, unraveling lace —
I let my hook go down, but I don't bite.
Everything comes back again, but
Not to the same place.

You gave a quiet to my touch.
Who could want the World-as-such?
All that nothing, an embrace —
Sometimes I appreciate what isn't so much.
Everything comes back again, but
Not to the same place.

And I suspect that whatever I know
Sprang up as weeds or scandals grow.
All that nothing, without a trace —
The way the wind and the money go,
Everything comes back again, but
Not to the same place.

GREAT CHAIN OF BEING

While I watch, filth collects on surfaces.
Noise and grease hang in the air like rain.
Unutterable what flows through streets and offices
Towards the black hole of the cosmic drain.

Lord, when You've looked at us and You're tired of what You're
    seeing,
Please do not neglect to pull the Great Chain of Being.

Great Chain of Being!
Great Great Great Chain of
Being!

Oh if I had it to do over, or just had it to do,
I'd probably make a mess of it, just like God.
Light stains the clear air a dirty shade of blue
While the daintiest foot is on its way to the meanest clod.

But everything is in order, from my individual peeing
To His final grinding tug on the Great Chain of Being.

Great Chain of Being!
Great Great Great Chain of
Being!

Do Not Disturb

If, when you've gotten past the door that's always locked,
Down the corridor they say is there, and if the passage isn't
blocked,
And if you find the stockroom where the things we want are
stocked,
Wake me then.

Or if you reach a cloudy gate, and if you make it through,
And if you find the treasuries of snow and rain and dew,
And bring back *all* the colors to replace our few,
Wake me then.

Or if you get across the ocean that's larger than our own,
And reach the fallen angels howling around their fallen throne,
And can tell me about their darkness, darker than I've known,
Wake me then.

Or if you come to a garden where a tree is blazing like ice,
A place in which even the most unique thing happens twice,
And if you're absolutely certain that it's free *and* Paradise,
Wake me then.

Or if, in your adventures, you should stumble on the place
From which all power flows like water pouring from a vase,
And then if, after seeing that, nothing else can ever be the case,
Wake me then.

Or if your plans wreck and go down, but if you keep
Exploring taste by taste the extreme flavors of the deep,
And if you come to rest in some more satisfying spot to sleep,
Wake me then.

FROM THE REAL SUBJECT:
QUERIES AND CONJECTURES OF JACOB DELAFON,
WITH SAMPLE POEMS

2004

Jacob Delafon reads: "To treat a fever, cut a cockchafer in two. Tape half of it to your right arm and the other half to your left."

He wonders about this.

What, actually, is a "cockchafer"? — he finds it a disturbing term.

He looks it up. It is a "pale-brown nocturnal beetle flying with a loud whirring sound."

All this is theoretical. Jacob has no fever.

•

Jacob Delafon reads, somewhere, that all human activity lies along two opposing vectors: the centrifugal push of paranoia and the centripetal pull of hysteria.

•

Jacob Delafon has read of a debate among doctors, as to whether nuns or prostitutes are more susceptible to hysteria.

•

Jacob Delafon locates the word *orthoepy*, meaning the "correct pronunciation of words." The word seems to him un-pronounceable.

•

Jacob Delafon, noting that Parsifal (like his cousin Lancelot) is a descendant of Joseph of Arimathea who, in turn, is of the House of David — in short, that Parsifal is a Jew — wonders if Wagner was aware of this.

WHIR

do not alarm yourself, I
could not rest content with
moral lectures and continual
repetition

like the solar system, I
could not hold my head up, made
endlessly to
glow

destined for grand ceremonies, I
was much affected by finding myself so
thin and so worn
down

(we use theory
to mean it is possible to
choose, e.g., why I am just the
size I am)

a million million, a
cool and mortifying manner — what
governs
motions

Jacob Delafon reads *A la recherche du temps perdu*.

In the last pages of the last volume, he finds the Past has been recaptured. The teeming World (i.e., the Novel) is now reduced to a single Character.

This must be, Jacob considers, hysteria's major text.

•

Jacob Delafon is surprised to read of ancient astronomers who "defied Time."

Later, he realizes it is a misprint for *deified*.

•

Time is something Jacob Delafon would prefer not to think about. But it does disturb him that while time seems — *moving image of eternity* — to slide around him somehow on its way elsewhere, at the same time ("Time," he mutters, "there it is again"), appears also completely at rest, standing absolutely still, while he himself plunges, or is plunged, through it.

•

Jacob Delafon is told that, after death, we will know nothing, but pain will continue. He regards this as unwarranted optimism.

•

His problem, Jacob Delafon decides, is how not to exist — without losing consciousness.

•

Jacob Delafon reads that, when painting the portrait of a living creature, it helps first to sketch the bones.

He cannot bring himself to start — Jane Floodcab posed before him — so likely it seems to him that he will never be up to adding vein or sinew, much less clothing the body with flesh and with skin.

·

Jacob Delafon is not sure what he thinks of life, but he is used to it.

·

This world, Jacob Delafon hears, is governed by angels.

He checks out a guide to Aquinas, the Angelic Doctor, and reads:

"There is nothing in an angel that might fall out, come loose, or be cut off."

"In their search for the kind of a body they needed, the angels were not reduced to grave-robbing. St. Thomas suggests, timidly, that the angels used compressed air as the material of these bodies. He was, of course, only guessing."

"Gabriel was not out of breath on his arrival in Nazareth."

·

Jacob Delafon turns the hour hand of his watch back one number, to standard time, a transition which, this year, falls oddly on Halloween.

Jacob hates daylight-saving time. He thinks daylight should be squandered.

·

Jacob Delafon is not sure what life thinks of him, but supposes it must be used to him.

•

Jacob Delafon likes to think of things in pairs: high and low, big and little, Mutt and Jeff, life and death, contagious and sympathetic, endocrine and peptide, Ungrund and Umwelt, aromatic rings and buckyballs…

•

Jacob Delafon has heard that scientific theories — statements involving the structure of the world — are judged, not only for consistency, but also for their formal elegance, for in fact a kind of beauty.

Jacob is bemused, the world, as he knows it, beautiful only in exceptions — only in its inconsistencies.

•

Jacob Delafon reads, attentively, "The Genesis of the Cat's Response to the Rat" by Zing Yang Kuo (1930).

Actually, what he reads, attentively, is a summary of this long article.

Kittens raised in a rat-killing environment, he learns, often turned out to be rat-killers.

Kittens raised in isolation sometimes killed rats, but a majority did not.

Killing a larger rat requires an older and larger cat.

"Vegetarianism had no effect on rat-killing, but had effect on rat-eating."

"The cat is a small-sized tiger."

"Do we need to add that in our findings the cat shows instincts of rat-killing and rat-eating as well as the instinct to love the rat?"

Aftertaste

half-unawakened

lost word

absorption of light and
scattering

startling
and

the place

this is how it
happens, every
night a little weaker

dreams of uncertain etymology

Jacob Delafon notes that Stefan Themerson classified the expression "good God" as an oxymoron.

Themerson, so far as Jacob remembers, never claimed there is no god, only that there is no god *to speak of*.

•

Jacob Delafon likes to quote scripture. To a business man he knows, for instance, he cries,

"Let thy companies deliver thee."

•

Jacob Delafon cannot remember where he read the warning

KEEP OUT OF REACH OF CHILDREN

but he has done his best always.

•

Jane Floodcab, finding Jacob, as is not infrequent, preoccupied, is wont to fling herself at him, crying out,

"Here I come, body or not."

•

"Why is it that bare feet are not good for sexual intercourse?"

"Why are men less capable of sexual intercourse in water?"

"Why is it that, if a living creature is born from our semen, we regard it as our own offspring, but if it proceeds from any other part or excretion, we do not consider it our own?"

"Why are those lustful whose eyelashes fall out?"

Jacob Delafon thinks Aristotle had problems.

"Why does tension and swelling of the penis occur? Is it because it is raised by the weight behind the testicles — the testicles acting as a fulcrum?"

•

Jacob Delafon is asked to picture a clockface. He represents it as the circle described by a sling's rotation.

His sling has no set target, no privileged zone, no firm persuasion.

Asked to explain why the hands come back to where they started, his mind wanders to the islands of an archipelago.

Archipelago

when rain arrives
the candle flame shivers
I have a habit of nothing

a charmed
life and a dozen
wounds
my blankets

when the train arrives
machine out of order
mind deranged
stomach upset
bowels loose
on that day I had not been asleep

support for a god or
perch for a bird
while
behind
time slides by

Jacob Delafon notes that the punishment of Adam and Eve was not what they had been threatened with: death. Their sentences were, instead, sweat and childbirth. They were condemned to live.

•

Jacob Delafon was impressed, even as a child, by how squirrels avoided him, not by running up a tree, but simply by scrambling to the other side of the trunk, out of his line of sight.

He wonders sometimes what other creatures, what other phenomena, so hide themselves.

•

Jacob Delafon, passing the Vedanta Society, notes this week's sermon topic: *Seeing God With Open Eyes.*

Jacob pauses to consider this, having always supposed it more common with eyes closed, usually after a blow on the head.

•

Walking, Jacob Delafon sees messages in the sidewalk, pressed into the cement before it hardened. Crude as the letters are, the words are legible.

"LEGALIZE HEMP," he reads, just across from Starbuck's.

Further on, "PLANT A TREE OR DIE."

•

Jacob Delafon's friend Mott laments the coming of old age. Jacob — the same age as his friend — insists that he, Jacob, has lost nothing to the years. He was, after all, never bold, never strong, never good looking.

And what could he do, back then, that he can not do now?

True, he concedes, after mature consideration, he can never, now, die young.

•

Jacob Delafon finds in Partridge's dictionary,

shit! mother, I can't dance

which, according to Partridge, means nothing at all, being simply what one says "just for something to say."

•

Jacob Delafon reads of an Arabic poetic form called *qasida* — which, according to some ninth century writer, may be about almost anything, but "should begin with the evocation of lost dwelling places and lost love, continue with the description of a journey, and culminate in the real subject."

In fact, the house where Jacob lives, and has lived for years, and where he will continue to live, he considers his lost home; Jane, in his arms, his lost love.

What he cannot seem to get to is a real subject.

2009

Shipwreck In Haven [6]

Behind and above, I saw then everything
that was happening on earth and can
describe the hum of clouds. Why

are you screaming? East of the sycamore
is the other world. Look: the same
road, lisp and rustle. At length you

may come to no decision, straight
as a die. Ample time for
dancing between acts. I am relieved

the sycamore is healthy — at my
death I will go to it. Not
*in*to it — but someday, if sufficiently

sensitive, you may
spot me, in the guise of child or
dwarf perhaps, leaning against the trunk like

a fallen branch. We are talking with
rhyme and reason, an art of
shading, smooth gradation

of loud and soft, velocity
distributed. Self-love, seeking
an object, splits

us in two. Nothing is
hidden from us, hour by
hour, with absolute certainty of its

occurrence. If I do
show up (perhaps as
dwarf or child) it will be to

the west — or south of the tree, *facing*
west. Children still of tender age are
taken into the forest and none of them

dare go home again, more and more
unfit for work, spending precious
time and learning nothing,

cantabile. You behold the wind coming
up the street. I doubt the easiness of
any access. Witness the horrors

of original scenery. First a
river. Then
a hill. What do you

bring that is good? The dead
pick these flowers and place them behind
their eyes and drink this water and have

no more desire. Good country near
the church. Twelve coffins
filled with shavings and in each

the little death pillow. The air is at
rest, belting around. Nothing
left for us to think about. Everything

proclaims the same language, not
the same thought. French windows, open
wide, flood the room with

regular patterns, like a military
parade. A large hall to
contain them. Pleasure at

every step. Soldiers swaying in the
breeze, their abundance and their
freedom. Counterblow to

night. I must devour you — skin,
hair and all. We must provide
for winter. Now let us examine

the dwellings of the kingdom
of heaven. What happens to
the severed parts? I hurl an axe

into the storm. Love potion: blood
dripping from the finger from one
year into the next. Hence my dread

of day's endless chain. When darkness
overtakes us, we will find no
shelter. I do not mind being

coachman on the box, but
drag you myself I
will not. Death is something

that occurs to a sleeper. Hair parted and
gathered in a Psyche knot back
of your head. Death

can strike the eye. Oh for me I
have other plans. Reason intervenes
to order impulse. Still, it

can appear — death — as
a solution, which of course
it is. Alone with your treasures,

hardly a budge to the little
ravine. Wild animals. Cry yourself
sleepy. I used to go to all

vampire films. Hope sprang
eternal. Lovers drink each
other's blood. First a river, then

a hill. A new vein opens. I
have admitted too many entities. Time
to razor down. I understand

how one might prefer to walk
bent over, eyes
to the pavement. We hear

horses neigh, soldiery laugh. Laid
waste, the farmers' fields. The cattle
killed. Men, women, slaughtered. Kings:

those that sleep. The king wears
a dragon mask. The king's soul
is lost and the king's soul is

found again. Dearest to each animal
its own constitution. Endless
causation. The king is not

what he seems to be. Death, disease,
weakness, being out of condition,
ugliness, and the like. If I

stir in my sleep, it is because the
point of a weapon has
touched us. It was my own

regard that quickened death, my
interest that made it personal.
Stories told by the fire at night making

creepy flesh, pneumatic
power, *cantabile*. You inspect
each one, lift it, put your

nose to it. Snow spreads a white
sheet over the grave. Will you
come? Verbatim. While wishing

still fulfills. Keep your eye
out for me, in the vicinity of
that tree. I will be

near it. Perhaps, in spring, as a child
reaching for the center. Look at the sycamore:
tall, healthy, flashing its regalia.

An Apparatus

From where I sit, I can see other
things: a silver porcupine, pins
standing upright. It is a vanished tale of a
vanished forest at the shore of a vanished ocean.

I call the dead as often as I can. In the
vaults, among mummies — this is pure
memorial. I am the girl in whose
eyes the name is written.

I feel as if veiled, as if soon I
shall get to know something. There are people
with encephalitis who cannot go
forward, but can go backward, and can dance.

In this rough draft of my memoirs, my brother
comes towards me — frightened, skeletal — longing
for marvels. I cannot describe it better than by
comparing it to other figures, intoxication.

Mere reflexes, as for instance breathing, can become
conscious. One of two rivals has his
ornamental tail bit off. In dying sounds, barely
reaching our ears, a melody continues.

No end to it — an infinite progression. All this
love of a bygone age. Watch the track
of a concentrated sunbeam through our lake ice:
part of the beam is stopped, part goes through.

Now the upper surface buckles, phantasmagoria of
unchained passion — under which the land
quakes, the ocean swells, and a myriad-years-
old forest snaps and cracks.

Surpassing all forms of experience, the wide, deep,
fresh water lake — on which the city
is built — rises before us. Here a modern idea
interposes, a new body made from the elements.

Then everything is forgotten. Sometimes thoughts
are cut off and sometimes they are the
blade which cuts. At the present gravel pit, electric
lights in the evening cast their magic blue sheen.

There's the sun, a crack above those
hills, breaking the day. If the door open, who
comes in? If it close, what will interrupt
my train?

The staircase effect supplies strong evidence
for a subjective map. Downhill, the sun
trickles, unperturbed. Here trots a mammoth with
red wool, through the black yew forest.

The tendency of elements to linger on: You say
I dream of what I want, but what I
want now is to dream. The cold rind
broken, the same wind blows.

Through a lens of ice, the dark
heat of the sun burns wood, fires gunpowder, melts
lead. Perhaps a cloud of musk arises, such as
issues from a crocodile in passion.

Unless light falls properly upon these
flowers, you cannot see them. All associations at
this level rain down from above. We
talk of word-pictures.

We observe vertigo. We reach the cleft
by a steep gully or *couloir* — very dangerous, the

path from the heights, the glory of
the prospect, the insight gained.

What I mean is a disturbance in
all the senses at once. You will not find
the flowers confused. Facing a certain
wind, there is always danger.

The Minimum Visible

Between the appearance of any
two ideas. Must
set the clock. Previously
future events. A little way back behind
moments. The spirit of a hawk.

In the future, the case
is altered. Intelligent trees
observing such a world the
sapling grows smaller. Gross
observation. Openly in full cry.

Successive acts in the direction
of the arrow. A short stretch already
past. Nothing in my direct
experience what is wrong?
This kind of trap survives.

Taking or has taken place
must be false, the narrow
now. Relived. Take-for-
granted may explode. Less:
thrash the wings.

Urging two senses at once suppose
I listen to a drum a two second
glissando they have any
bearing on our normal ex-
perience. Recall the hounds.

Within interval of physical space the
theory elusive. Con-
founding pulsational. Hold
the pendulum. Trail. The hollow
shaft of the feather.

Plurality of Worlds

And each inhabited. And each
inhabitant resolves. And I, I with
my various processes. I stumble, I
revolve.

As one
sees, in the desert, water
welling, always distant, forever
unapproachable.

A view of the chase
from the battlements. To see something — any-
thing — I always step back. And then:
where am I?

Distant. Unapproachable. My
name. Jericho. Absurdly — I mean, out of
tune. And forgetfulness? deceit?
error?

For us to grow
old, the moon must rise. From invisible
fire, flames leap into view. A dream
of bodily heaven.

Hot colors, subtle
nuances. Motives recast in site
after site. Figures absorbed by
a plethora of drapery.

I must remove all this:
evening chill, an impression of transparency, your
presence — remove it all, without
letting anything go.

I was born in December
and things seem always to come at me like
January. The fifty-third bird in the
tree this morning.

Joy, laughter,
lamentation — it's like a map. Minuet.
Waltz. Ninety percent too
dark to see.

Let me think now. Roads.
Tombs. Temples. I could list my
friends... What will I
forget next?

Light, analyzed by
dusk, and then? The spectres
still there. A painterly softening. Almost
heraldic poses.

Long narrow
slits of light, dark bars against bright
ground, or straight-line borders peculiarly
oriented.

Looking one way, everything
is lost. The other direction: nothing to
lose. In a crystal I glimpse, maybe, my
waking state.

My soul's
fictitious body... Think. My
health: the world's long
lingering illness.

Pain, hot-cold, mere
contact. Crude sensory modalities. These

remain after destruction of the sensory
cortex. Pain.

Shock waves. Feathery
feet of barnacles. It does not
reach us, the sun's bottomless
profundo.

Things age and, when old
enough, no longer able to resist,
become animate. Unable to stay
free of life.

What remains of
ancient rites? Grammar. I
would never give up anything I have, in
return for mere certainty.

Natural Colors

With regard to
the point of sight and the
divergence of visual rays, a faithful
representation is
given, though drawn on a
flat façade: some parts
withdrawing, others
standing in relief.

First prize to the poet who
least pleases his audience.

Let the kitchen be warm.

Let oxen face only the direction of
sunrise and not
pass in envious silence.

Something happens.

STONE ANGELS
Swan Point Cemetery, Providence, Rhode Island

for Barton Levi St.Armand

Angels go — we

merely stray, image of
a wandering deity, searching for
wells or for work. They scale
rungs of air, ascending
and descending — we are a little
lower. The grass covers us.

But statues, here, they stand, simple as
horizon. Statements,
yes — but what they stand for
is long fallen.

Angels of memory: they point
to the death of time, not
themselves timeless, and without
recall. Their
strength is to stand
still, afterglow
of an old religion.

One can imagine them
sentient — that is to say, we may
attribute to stone-hardness, one after the
other, our own five senses, until it spring
to life and
breathe and sneeze and step
down among us.

But in fact, they are
the opposite of perception: we
bury our gaze in them. For all my
sympathy, I
suppose they see
nothing at all, eyeless to indicate
our calamity, breathless and graceful
above the ruins they inspire.

I could close my eyes now and
evade, maybe, the blind
fear that their wings hold.

The visible body expresses our
body as a whole, its
internal asymmetries, and also the broken
symmetry we wander through.

With practice I might
regard people and things — the field
around me — as blots: objects
for fantasy, shadowy but
legible. All these
words have other meanings. A little
written may be far too
much to read.

A while and a while and a while, after a
while make something like forever.

From ontological bric-a-brac, and
without knowing quite what they
mean, I select my
four ambassadors: my
double, my shadow, my shining
covering, my name.

The graven names are not their
names, but ours.

Expectation, endlessly
engraved, is a question
to beg. Blemishes on exposed
surfaces — perpetual
corrosion — enliven features
fastened to the stone.

Expecting nothing without
struggle, I come to expect nothing
but struggle.

The primal Adam, our
archetype — light at his back, heavy
substance below him — glanced
down into uncertain depths, fell in
love with and fell
into his own shadow.

Legend or history: footprints
of passing events. Lord,
how our information
increaseth.

I see only
a surface — complex enough, its
interruptions of
deep blue — suggesting that the earth
is hollow, stretched around
what must be *all the rest*.

My 'world' is parsimonious — a few
elements which
combine, like tricks of light, to

sketch the barest outline. But my
void is lavish, breaking
its frame, tempting me always to
turn again, again, for each
glimpse suggests more and more in some
other, farther emptiness.

To reach empty space, think
away each object — without destroying
its position. Ghostly then, with
contents gone, the
vacuum will not, as you
might expect, collapse, but
hang there,
vacant, waiting an inrush of
reappointments seven times
worse than anything you know, seven other dimensions
curled into our three.

But time empties, on
occasion, more quickly than
that. Breathe in or out. No
motion moves.

Trees go down, random and
planted, the
way we think.

The sacrificial animal is
consumed by fire, ascends in greasy
smoke, an offering
to the sky. Earthly
refuse assaults
heaven, as we are contaminated by
notions of eternity. It is as if
a love letter — or everything I

have written — were to be
torn up and the pieces
scattered, in
order to reach the beloved.
No entrance after
sundown. Under how vast a
night, what we
call day.

What stands still is merely
extended — what
moves is in space.

Immobile figures, here, in a
race with death, gloom about their
heads like a dark nimbus.

Still, they do — while standing —
go: they've a motion
like the flow of water, like
ice, only slower. Our
time is a river, theirs
the glassy sea.

They drift, as
we do, in this garden so swank, so grandly
indiscriminate. Frail
wings, fingers too fragile. Their faces
freckle, weathering.

Pure spirit, saith the Angelic
Doctor. But not these
angels: pure visibility, hovering,
lifting horror into the day,
to cancel and preserve it.

The worst death, worse
than death, would be to die, leaving
nothing unfinished.
Somewhere in my life, there
must have been — buried now under
long accumulation — some extreme
joy which, never spoken, cannot
be brought to mind. How else, in this
unconscious city, could I have
such a sense of dwelling?

I would
raise…What's the opposite
of Ebenezer?

Night, with its crypt, its
cradle-song. Rage
for day's end: impatience,
like a boat in the evening. Towards
the horizon, as
down a sounding line. Barcarolle,
funeral march.

Nocturne at high noon.

FROM THE NOT FOREVER

2013

Also a Fountain
[re-buildings]

i.

He broke the bread, in not quite normal Greek…

There was once a traveler lost his way.

…indeed our body

Spotted a farmhouse, went up and knocked..Woman came to the door..
Invited him in.

…lest fragments be lost…

Seemed no one there, except this woman — and two pretty girls.. He
was welcomed.. Given food and drink.. Later shown to a bed.

…animistic…. sinister…

The man asked if he might sleep with one of the girls..Was told that
he could.

…horror…. blood applied, not to doorposts, not to lintel, but
to the lips…

Man took off his clothes and the girl hers..The man lay down and the
girl lay down beside him.

…wand raised…. baskets of loaves or…. water-pots…

Turned towards her, he could feel no body.

…likeness…

He caught hold of her, embraced her.. He held her in his arms, but in his arms felt nothing — though all the while she lay beside him.. He could see her perfectly well.

...antitype...

She said, "I am a spirit."

...*figura*.... name of assumed flesh.... elixir of immortality.... death's antidote...

"Bodiless," she said.

(silent signifiers...

She said, "I cannot give you pleasure."

...unmarked practices)

Body ascends by sense.. Spirit descends into sense.

...the body as a scale, leading upwards.... downwards.... leading anywhere.... nowhere.... flight hindered...

...dictionaries, their weight...

...as always...

...dying

ii.

...his forehead, coming
up and poking, works

the top-
notch, seems
very strange

thinks it best never
touch a cent, knows
little about art, must

obtain those pictures, looks
doubtful, calls to
one of the waiters

has never
taken time

nods cropped
head, sort of
figures

stands against the door, moves
warningly
flops flat on his face

doesn't
know, looks up, wincing
certainly cannot

wipes...

iii.

When the palace was rebuilt, the pictures, burned along with so much else — flammable details of a pile given to the flames — had to be painted again.. Painted, necessarily, by artists not from those past times the pictures came from.

And (given the years that had passed) not by any who had actually seen the pictures.

When the king was renamed, the body had to be made over, words replaced by frenzy, blood raised to natural heat.

My state, most unfortunate: a light sleeper who finds it impossible to stay awake.

When the story was retold, near a hermitage on a wild coast, a wedding was in progress.. Warriors in wild dance, fleeing with their wounded leader.

Conversation overheard.. Broad staircase unobserved.. Great hall.. People applauding.. The marriage postponed.

When the idea returned, a book written on separate leaves, each leaf contained five hundred characters.. A victorious king concealed his joy in prison.

Long.

Sad.

Frozen.

Ruined tower.

Ache of distance.

Pictures of terror.

Being above.. Beam.. Boom.. Bumpkin.

His daughter Christina.. Christina in disguise.
Whose daughter?

Harbor.

When the road was put through, two kings, by their embellishments (for example: a veneer of blue enamelled bricks), invested it with a splendour which made it the wonder of their world..

Public square.. Court.. Tower.

Fishermen's quarter.

Bonding the bricks with reeds.

Stockholm? Leipzig? Alexandria? Attack prepared.

When all this was done, where am I?

Attack.

Which is to say, who am I?

News of treason.

Ship explodes.

To save the city.. To flee in her cloak.. To be aware.

To make aware.

Awake?

iv.

A relativity of the taut string.

Afterword

Keith Waldrop is a quiet major poet, a major poet of quiet. His accomplishment is difficult to describe because his work refuses, in Bartelby-like fashion, the twin traps of impassivity and affectation: "On my one hand, / stasis — on the / other, striving for effect." In one of his very few interviews, Waldrop says: "I think the worst fault a poem can have is striving for effect." Waldrop never strives; instead, he haunts—his presence is all the more powerful for barely being there, like a ghost you discover in a familiar photograph. There are plenty of direct statements, moments of humor and pathos, but we come to know Waldrop most through his subtle, exquisite compositional decisions: the way he breaks a line or collages found language. I think here of the perfectly balanced epigrammatic poem "Proposition II":

> Each grain of sand has its architecture, but
> a desert displays the structure of the wind.

I read the poem as a tiny *ars poetica*: Waldrop has composed two lines of eleven syllables each—syllables of sound/sand whose arrangement displays the structure of Waldrop's thinking just as a drift makes visible the activity of the wind. We intuit the author from the architecture, from the traces he has left.

Ghosts are everywhere in Waldrop's work, but they're not supernatural occurrences: a ghost for Waldrop is more a felt absence than a felt presence. As he wrote in his brilliant autobiographical novel, *Light While There Is Light*—recently reissued by Dalkey Archive—"my ghosts merely disappear. I never see them. They haunt me by not being there, by the table where no one eats, the empty window that lets the sun in without a shadow." In his first published book of poems,

A Windmill Near Calvary, Waldrop echoes this sentiment: "The terrible thing about / ghosts is that we know they are not there." That's a fine shorthand for Waldrop's gentle but rigorous skepticism: his poems explore the desire for something beyond the visible, and confront the nothing that is there. But that's not just a journey of despair; it's also a recovery of wonder before the actual world—each grain of sand, and the relations between grains.

In a poem in *Windfall Losses*—only now do I see the "structure of the wind" in Waldrop's titles—he calls for a "phenomenology of ignorance," and in part that's what this volume is: a beautiful, delicate, and various exploration of the endless (and so objectless) activities of thinking and feeling, the truth always just out of reach. Activity over stasis, but ignorance over false effects. It's rather surprising that Waldrop—perhaps the most erudite writer I know—should so often avow his ignorance, but that position of unknowing has allowed him to see and sound what would escape the perception of the more egotistical poet. Sometimes reading Waldrop I feel like I'm attending a séance. No ghosts appear, but the mundane objects—both the things words are and the things words describe—start to stir a little, start to glow. "Loved houses are haunted," ends the poem from *A Windmill Near Calvary* I quoted above. "And I have / no explanation."

—Ben Lerner

photo by Connie Grosch

KEITH WALDROP (born Emporia, Kansas, 1932) retired from Brown University in Providence, RI, where he still lives and, with Rosmarie Waldrop, is editor of the small press, Burning Deck.

His recent poetry books are *The Not Forever* (Omnidawn), *Transcendental Studies* (University of California Press, National Book Award 2009), *The Real Subject* (Omnidawn) and a trilogy: *The Locality Principle*, *The Silhouette of the Bridge*, and *Semiramis If I Remember* (Avec Books). Siglio has published a book of collages, *Several Gravities*. His novel, *Light While There Is Light*, has been reissued by Dalkey Archive.

He has translated Baudelaire's *Flowers of Evil* and *Paris Spleen* (Wesleyan University Press) as well as books by contemporary French poets Anne-Marie Albiach, Claude Royet-Journoud, Paol Keineg, Dominique Fourcade, Pascal Quignard, and Jean Grosjean.

Selected Poems
by Keith Waldrop

Cover text set in Joanna MT Std.
Interior text set in Perpetua Std.

Original cover collage by Keith Waldrop

Cover and interior design by Cassandra Smith of Molo Projects
www.moloprojects.org

Offset printed in the United States
by Edwards Brothers Malloy, Ann Arbor, Michigan
On 55# Enviro Natural 100% Recycled 100% PCW
Acid Free Archival Quality FSC Certified Paper

Publication of this book was made possible in part by gifts from:
Robin & Curt Caton
John Gravendyk

Omnidawn Publishing
Richmond, California
2016

Rusty Morrison & Ken Keegan, senior editors & co-publishers
Gillian Olivia Blythe Hamel, managing editor
Melissa Burke, marketing manager
Cassandra Smith, poetry editor & book designer
Peter Burghardt, poetry editor & book designer
Sharon Zetter, poetry editor, book designer & development officer
Liza Flum, poetry editor & marketing assistant
Juliana Paslay, fiction editor
Gail Aronson, fiction editor
RJ Ingram, *OmniVerse* contributing editor
Kevin Peters, marketing assistant & *OmniVerse* Lit Scene editor
Trisha Peck, marketing assistant
Sara Burant, administrative assistant
Josie Gallup, publicity assistant
SD Sumner, publicity assistant